Mother Goose

Ride a Cock-horse.

Mother Goose's Nursery Rhymes

Robert Frederick • Publishers

To see the Queen.

Introduction.

"MAY I have the pleasure to introduce
Some very old friends?" says Mother Goose.

"There's little Bo-Peep and little Boy Blue,
The little old Woman who lived in a shoe,

Old Mother Hubbard as well as her dog,
Dame Trot and Sir Anthony Rowley Frog,

Humpty Dumpty, and Dickory Dock,
The dear little mouse who ran up the clock,

The puss who journeyed to London alone,
And saw the queen on a golden throne:

So come, my little folks, open me,
And lots of other old friends you'll see!"

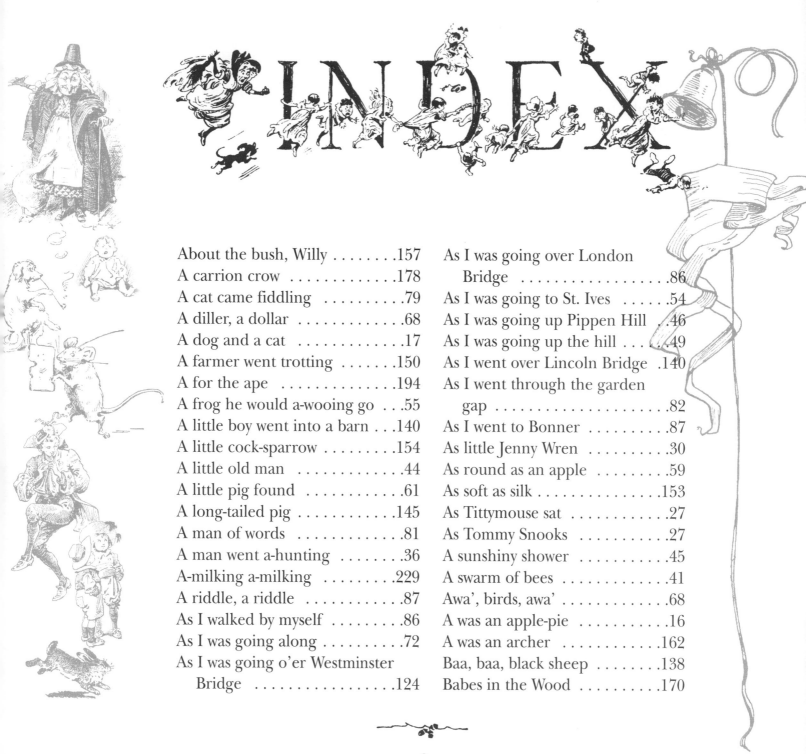

INDEX

LONGER STORIES

THERE was
a little man,
And he had
a little gun,
And his bullets
were made
of lead, lead, lead;
He went to the brook,
And saw a little duck,
And shot it through
the head, head, head.

He carried it home to his old wife Joan,
And bade her a fire to make, make, make,
To roast the little duck
He had shot in the brook,
And he'd go and fetch
the drake, drake, drake.

Mother Goose's Nursery Rhymes.

Dickory, Dickory, Dock.

DICKORY, dickory, dock,
   The mouse ran up the clock,
   The clock struck one,
The mouse ran down;
   Hickory, dickory, dock.

There was An Old Man.

THERE was an old man,
And he had a calf,
 And that's half;
He took him out of the stall,
And put him on the wall,
 And that's all.

There Was a Crooked Man.

THERE was a crooked man, and he went a crooked mile,
He found a crooked sixpence against a crooked stile:
he bought a crooked cat, which caught a crooked mouse,
And they all lived together in a little crooked house.

Little Bo-Peep.

LITTLE Bo-peep has lost her sheep,
    And can't tell where to find them;
Leave them alone, and they'll come home,
    And bring their tails behind them.

Little Bo-peep fell fast asleep,
    And dreamed she heard them bleating;
But when she awoke, she found it a joke,
    For they were still a-fleeting.

Then up she took her little crook,
    Determined for to find them;
She found them indeed,
    But it made.her heart bleed,
For they'd left all their tails behind 'em.

Peter Piper.

PETER PIPER picked a peck of pickled peppers;
A peck of pickled peppers Peter Piper picked;
If Peter Piper picked a peck of pickled peppers,
Where's the peck of pickled peppers Peter Piper picked?

Little Bo-Peep.

A was an Apple Pie

A was an apple-pie;
B bit it;
C cut it;
D dealt it;
E eat it;
F fought for it;
G got it;
H had it;
J joined it;
K kept it;
L longed for it;
M mourned for it;
N nodded at it;
O opened it;
P peeped in it;
Q quartered it;
R ran for it;
S stole it;
T took it;
V viewed it;
W wanted it;
X, Y, Z, and Amperse-And
All wished for a piece in hand.

A Dog and a Cat
Went Out Together.

A DOG and a cat went out together,
   To see some friends just out of town;
      Said the cat to the dog,
      "What d'ye think of the weather?"
   "I think, ma'am, the rain will come down;
   But don't be alarmed, for I've an umbrella
   That will shelter us both," said this amiable fellow.

"What will the children do then, poor things?"

This is the Way.

THIS is the way the ladies ride;
   Tri, tre, tre, tree,
   Tri, tre, tre, tree!
This is the way the ladies ride,
    Tri, tre, tre, tre, tri, tre, tre, tree!

This is the way the gentlemen ride;
   Gallop-a-trot,
   Gallop-a-trot!
This is the way the gentlemen ride,
   Gallop-a-trot-a-trot!

This is the way the farmers ride;
   Hobbledy-hoy,
   Hobbledy-hoy!
This is the way the farmers ride,
   Hobbledy-hobbledy-hoy!

The North Wind.

THE north wind doth blow,
And we shall have snow,
And what will the robin do then,
    Poor thing?

He'll sit in the barn
And keep himself warm,
And hide his head under his wing,
    Poor thing.

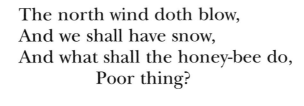

The north wind doth blow,
And we shall have snow,
And what shall the honey-bee do,
        Poor thing?

In his hive he will stay
Till the cold's passed away,
And then he'll come out in the spring,
        Poor thing.

The north wind doth blow,
And we shall have snow,
And what will the dormouse do then,
        Poor thing?

Rolled up like a ball
In his nest snug and small,
He'll sleep till warm weather comes back,
        Poor thing.

The north wind doth blow,
And we shall have snow,
And what will the children do then,
        Poor things?

When lessons are done,
They'll jump, skip, and run,
And that's how they'll keep themselves warm,
        Poor things.

"The north wind doth blow."

The Old Woman and Her Pig.

AN old woman was sweeping her house, and she found a little crooked sixpence. "What," said she, "shall do with this little sixpence? I will go to market, and buy a little pig." As she was coming home, she came to a stile; the piggy would not go over the stile.

She went a little farther, and she met a dog. So she said to the dog—

> "Dog, dog, bite pig;
> Piggy won't get over the stile;
> And I shan't get home to-night."

But the dog would not.
She went a little farther, and she met a stick. So she said—

"Stick, stick, beat dog;
Dog won't bite pig;
Piggy won't get over the stile;
And I shan't get home to-night."

But the stick would not. She
went a little farther, and she met
a fire. So she said—

"Fire, fire, burn stick;
Stick won't beat dog;
Dog won't bite pig;
Piggy won't get over the stile;
And I shan't get home to-night."

But the fire would not.

She went a little farther, and she met some water. So she said—

> "Water, water, quench fire;
> Fire won't burn stick ;" etc.

But the water would not.

She went a little farther, and she met an Ox. So she said—

> "Ox ox , drink water;
> Water won't quench fire;" etc.

But the ox would not.

She went a little farther and she met a butcher. So she said—

"Butcher, butcher, kill ox;
Ox won't drink water;" etc.

But the butcher would not. She went a little farther, and she met a rope. So she said—

"Rope, rope, hang butcher;
Butcher won't kill ox ;" etc.

But the rope would not. She went a little farther, and she met a rat. So she said—

"Rat, rat gnaw rope;
Rope won't hang butcher;" etc.

But the rat would not.
She went a little farther, and she met a cat. So she said—

"Cat, cat, kill rat;
Rat won't gnaw rope ;" etc.

But the cat said to her, "If you will go to yonder cow, and fetch me a saucer of milk, I will kill the rat." So away went the old woman to the cow, and said—

"Cow, cow, give me a saucer of milk;
Cat won't kill rat ;" etc.

But the cow said to her, "If you will go to yonder hay-makers, and fetch me a wisp of hay, I'll give you the milk." So away went the old woman to the hay-makers, and said—

"Haymakers, give me a wisp of hay;
Cow won't give me milk ;" etc.

But the haymakers said to her, "If you will go to yonder stream, and fetch us a bucket of water, we'll give you the hay." So away the old woman went; but when she got to the stream, she found the bucket was full of holes. So she covered the bottom with pebbles, and then filled the bucket with water, and away she went back with it to the haymakers; and they gave her a wisp of hay. As soon as the cow had eaten the hay, she gave the old woman the milk; and away she went with it in a saucer to the cat. As soon as the cat had lapped up the milk;—

The cat began to kill the rat;
The rat began to gnaw the rope;
The rope began to hang the butcher;
The butcher began to kill the ox
The ox began to drink the water;
The water began to quench the fire;
The fire began to burn the stick;
The stick began to beat the dog
The dog began to bite the pig;
The pig in a fright jumped over the stile;
And so the old woman got home that night.

As Tommy Snooks.

AS Tommy Snooks and Bessy Brooks
 Were walking out one Sunday,
Says Tommy Snooks to Bessy Brooks,
 "To-morrow will be Monday."

As Tittymouse sat.

As Tittymouse sat in the witty to spin,
Pussy came to her and bid her good e'en.
"Oh what are you doing, my little 'oman?"
"A-spinning a doublet for my gude man."
"Then shall I come to thee and wind up thy thread?"
"Oh no, Mr. Puss, you will bite off my head."

Little Jack Horner.

Little Jack Horner.

LITTLE JACK Horner
Sat in the corner,
  Eating a Christmas pie;
He put in his thumb,
And he took out a plum,
  And said, "What a good boy am I!"

If I'd as Much Money.

IF I'd as much money as I could spend;
I never would cry old chairs to mend;
Old chairs to mend, old chairs to mend;
I never would cry old chairs to mend.

If I'd as much money as I could tell;
I never would cry old clothes to sell;
Old clothes to sell, old clothes to sell;
I never would cry old clothes to sell.

Pretty John Watts.

PRETTY John Watts,
We are troubled with rats,
Will you drive them out of the house?
We have mice too, in plenty,
That feast in the pantry;
But let them stay
And nibble away
What harm in a little brown mouse?

As Little Jenny Wren.

AS little Jenny Wren
    Was sitting by the shed,
She waggled with her tail,
    And nodded with her head.
She waggled with her tail,
    And nodded with her head,
As little Jenny Wren
    Was sitting by the shed.

Bow-wow, says the Dog.

Bow-wow, says the dog;
  Mew, mew, says the cat;
Grunt, grunt, goes the hog;
  And squeak goes the rat.

Tu-whu, says the owl;
  Caw, caw, says the crow;
Quack, quack, says the duck;
  And what sparrows say you know.

So, with sparrows, and owls,
  With rats, and with dogs,
With ducks, and with crows,
  With cats, and with hogs,

A fine song I have made,
  To please you, my dear;
And if it's well sung,
  'Twill be charming to hear.

I had a little Hobby Horse.

I HAD a little hobby horse,
   And it was dapple gray;
Its head was made of pea straw.
    Its tail was made of hay.
I sold it to an old woman
   For a copper groat;
And I'll not sing my song again
    Without a new coat.

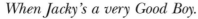

When Jacky's a very Good Boy.

WHEN Jacky's a very a good boy,
   He shall have cakes and a custard,
But when he does nothing but cry,
   He shall have nothing but mustard.

Bessy Bell and Mary Gray.

BESSY BELL and Mary Gray,
   They were two bonny lasses;
They built their house upon the lea,
   And covered it with rashes.
Bessy kept the garden gate,
   And Mary kept the pantry;
Bessy always had to wait,
   While Mary lived in plenty.

Dickery, dickery, dare.

DICKERY, dickery, dare,
   The pig flew up in the air;
The man in brown soon brought him down,
   Dickery, dickery, dare.

Cross-patch, Draw the Latch.

CROSS-PATCH,
   Draw the latch,
Sit by the fire and spin;
   Take a cup,
And drink it up,
   Then call your neighbours in.

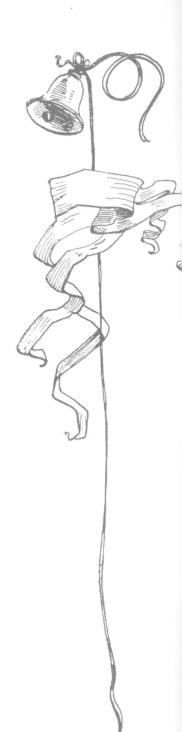

GIRLS
and boys,
come out
to play,
The moon doth
shine as bright as day;

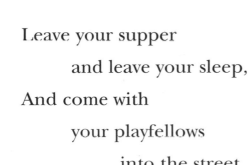

Leave your supper
and leave your sleep,
And come with
your playfellows
into the street.

Come with a whoop,
come with a call,
Come with good will.
or not at all.

Up the ladder and down the wall,
A halfpenny roll will serve us all.
You find milk, and I'll find flour,
And we'll have a pudding in half an hour.

Lend Me thy Mare.

"L END me thy mare to ride a mile?"
"She is lamed, leaping over a stile."
"Alack! and I must keep the fair!
I'll give thee money for thy mare."
"Oh, oh, say you so?
Money will make the mare to go!"

Little Bob Snooks.

LITTLE Bob Snooks was fond of his books,
     And loved by his usher and master;
But naughty Jack Spry, he got a black eye,
     And carries his nose in a plaster.

If You Sneeze on a Monday.

IF YOU sneeze on Monday, you sneeze for danger;
Sneeze on a Tuesday, kiss a stranger;
Sneeze on a Wednesday, sneeze for a letter;
Sneeze on a Thursday, something better;
Sneeze on a Friday, sneeze for sorrow;
Sneeze on a Saturday, see your sweetheart to-morrow.

Higglepy, Piggleby

Higglepy, Piggleby,
  My black hen,
She lays eggs
  For gentlemen;
Sometimes nine,
  And sometimes ten,
Higglepy, Piggleby,
  My black hen!

A Man went a-Hunting.

A MAN went a-hunting at Reigate,
  And wished to leap over a high gate;
Says the owner, "Go round!
  With your gun and your hound,
For you never shall jump over my gate."

I love Sixpence, Pretty Little Sixpence.

I LOVE sixpence, pretty little sixpence,
  I love sixpence better than my life;
I spent a penny of it, I spent another,
  And I took fourpence home to my wife.

Oh, my little four pence, pretty little fourpence,
  I love fourpence better than my life;
I spent a penny of it, I spent another,
  And I took twopence home to my wife.

Oh, my little twopence, my pretty little twopence,
  I love twopence better than my life;
I spent a penny of it, I spent another,
  And I took nothing home to my wife.

Oh, my little nothing, my pretty little nothing,
  What will nothing buy for my wife?
I have nothing, I spend nothing,
  I love nothing better than my wife.

The Man in the Moon.

THE man in the Moon
Came tumbling down,
And asked his
way to Norwich;
He went by
the south,
And burnt his mouth,
With supping cold
pease-porridge.

Oranges and Lemons.

GAY go up, and gay go down,
To ring the bells of London town.

Bull's eyes and targets,
Say the bells of St. Marg'ret's.

Brickbats and tiles,
Say the bells of St. Giles'.

Halfpence and farthings,
Say the bells of St. Martin's.

Oranges and lemons,
Say the bells of St. Clement's.

LITTLE Tom Tucker
Sings for his supper;
What shall he eat?
White bread and butter.
How shall he cut it
Without e'er a knife?
How will he be married
Without e'er a wife?

Oranges and Lemons (continued).

Pancakes and fritters,
Say the bells of St. Peter's.

Two sticks and an apple,
Say the bells at Whitechapel.

Old Father Baldpate,
Say the slow bells at Aldgate.

Pokers and tongs,
Say the bells at St. John's.

Kettles and pans,
Say the bells at St. Ann's.

You owe me ten shillings,
Say the bells at St. Helen's.

When will you pay me?
Say the bells at Old Bailey.

When I grow rich,
Say the bells at Shoreditch.

Pray, when will that be?
Say the bells of Stepney.

I am sure I don't know,
Says the great bell at Bow.

Here comes a candle to light you to bed,
And here comes a chopper to chop off your head.

Buff says Buff.

BUFF says Buff to all his men,
And I say Buff to you again;
Buff neither laughs nor smiles,
But carries his face
With a very good grace,
And passes the stick to the very next place!

Hark, hark! the Dogs do Bark!

HARK, hark!
The dogs do bark,
The beggars are coming to town
Some in rags,
Some in jags,
And some in velvet gowns.

A Swarm of Bees in May.

A SWARM of Bees in May
Is worth a load of hay;
A swarm of bees in June
Is worth a silver spoon;
A swarm of bees in July
Is not worth a fly.

For Want of a Nail.

FOR want of a nail, the shoe was lost,
For want of the shoe, the horse was lost,
For want of the horse, the rider was lost,
For want of the rider, the battle was lost,
For want of the battle, the kingdom was lost,
And all from the want of a horseshoe nail !

Fiddle-de-dee.

FIDDLE-DE-DEE, fiddle de dee,
The fly shall marry the humble-bee.
They went to the church, and married was she,
The fly has married the humble-bee.

Elizabeth, Elspeth.

ELIZABETH, Elspeth, Betsy, and Bess,
They all went together to seek a bird's nest.
They found a bird's nest with five eggs in,
They all took one, and left four in.

Little Miss Muffet.

LITTLE Miss Muffet
   Sat on a tuffet,
Eating of curds and whey;
   There came a spider,
   And sat down beside her,
And frightened Miss Muffet away.

My Lady Wind, my Lady Wind.

My Lady Wind, my Lady wind,
Went round about the house to find
   A chink to get her foot in.
   She tried the key-hole in the door,
She tried the crevice in the floor,
And drove the chimney soot in.

And then one night when it was dark,
She blew up such a tiny spark,
   That all the house was bothered:
From it she raised up such a flame,
As flamed away to Belting Lane,
   And White Cross folks were smothered.

And thus when once, my little dears,
A whisper reaches itching ears,
   The same will come, you'll find:
Take my advice, restrain the tongue,
Remember what old Nurse has sung
   Of busy Lady Wind!

Little Miss Muffet.

Jacky, come, give Me thy Fiddle.

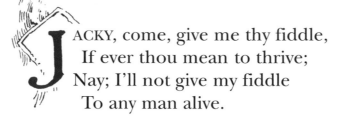

JACKY, come, give me thy fiddle,
  If ever thou mean to thrive;
Nay; I'll not give my fiddle
  To any man alive.

If I should give my fiddle,
  They'll think that I'm gone mad;
For many a joyful day
  My fiddle and I have had.

A Little Old Old Man.

A LITTLE old man of Derby,
How do you think he served me?
He took away my bread and cheese,
And that is how he served me.

The Sow came in with the Saddle.

THE SOW came in with the saddle,
The little Pig rocked the cradle,
The Dish jumped on the table,
To see the Pot swallow the Ladle.
The Spit that stood behind the door
Threw the Pudding-stick on the floor.
"Odsplut! "said the Gridiron, "can't you agree?
I'm the head constable,— bring them to me."

A Sunshiny Shower.

A SUNSHINY Shower
Won't last half an hour.

Some Little Mice Sat.

SOME little mice sat in a barn to spin;
Pussy came by, and popped her head in;
"Shall I come in, and cut your threads off?"
"Oh! no, kind sir, you could snap our heads off."

45

I had a Little Nut-tree.

I HAD a little nut-tree; nothing would it bear
But a silver nutmeg and a golden pear;
The King of Spain's daughter came to visit me
And all because of my little nut-tree.
I skipped over water, I danced over sea,
And all the birds in the air couldn't catch me.

If Ifs and Ands.

IF ifs and ands
Were pots and pans,
There would be no need for tinkers!

Come when You're Called.

COME when you're called,
Do What you're bid,
Shut the door after you,
Never be chid.

As I was Going Up Pippen Hill.

As I was going up Pippen Hill—,
Pippen Hill was dirty,—,
There I met a pretty miss,
And she dropped me a curtsey.

Little miss, pretty miss,
Blessings light upon you!
If I had half-a-crown a day,
I'd spend it all upon you.

THE fox and his wife they had a great strife,
They never ate mustard in all their whole life;
They ate their meat without fork or knife,
    And loved to be picking a bone, e-ho!

The fox jumped up on a moonlight night;
The stars they were shining, and all things bright;
'O ho!" said the fox, "it's a very fine night
    For me to go through the town, e-ho!"

The fox, when he came to yonder stile,
He lifted his lugs and he listened a while!
"'O ho!" said the fox, "it's but a short mile
    From this unto yonder wee town, e-ho!"

The fox, when he came to the farmer's gate,
Who should he see but the farmer's drake;
"I love you well for your master's sake,
    And long to be picking your bone, e-ho!"

The grey goose
      she ran
    round the hay-stack,
    "Oho!" said the fox,
      "you are very fat;
You'll grease my beard,
and ride on my back
    From this
unto yonder wee town,
      e-ho !"

Old Gammer Hipple-hopple
      hopped out of bed,
      she opened the casement,
      and popped out
        her head:
      "Oh husband! Oh husband!
        the grey goose is dead
And the fox has gone
        through the town O!"

Then the old man got up in his red cap,
And swore he would catch the fox in a trap;
But the fox was too cunning, and gave him the slip
    And ran through the town, the town, O!

When he got to the top of the hill,
He blew his trumpet both loud and shrill,
For joy that he was safe
    Through the town, O!

When the fox came back to his den,
He had young ones both nine and ten,
"You're welcome home, daddy, you may go again,
If you bring us such nice meat
    From the town, O!"

As I was Going up the Hill.

As I was going up the hill,
    I met with Jack the piper,
And all the tune that he could play
    was, "Tie up your petticoats tighter."

I tied them once, I tied them twice,
    I tied them three times over;
And all the song that he could sing
    Was, "Carry me safe to Dover."

Bryan O'Lin

BRYAN O'LIN, and his wife, and wife's mother,
They all went over the bridge together;
The bridge was broken, and they all fell in—
"The deuce go with all!" quoth Bryan O'Lin.

Buz, quoth the Blue Fly.

BUZ, quoth the blue fly,
   Hum, quoth the bee;
Buz and hum, they Cry,
   And so do we.
In his ear, in his nose,
   Thus, do you see?
He ate the dormouse,
   Else it was he.

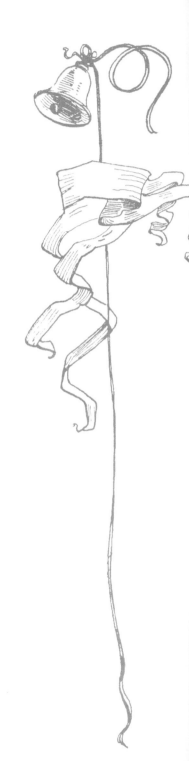

He that would Thrive.

HE that would thrive
   Must rise at five;
He that hath thriven
   May lie till seven;
And he that by the plough would thrive,
Himself must either hold or drive.

I Doubt, I Doubt.

I DOUBT, I doubt my fire's all out,
My little dame is not at home?
I'll saddle my cock, and bridle my hen,
And fetch my little dame home again!

Doctor Faustus.

DOCTOR FAUSTUS was a good man
    He whipped his scholars now and then;
    When he whipped them, he made them dance
    Out of Scotland into France,
    Out of France into Spain,
    And then he whipped them back again!

Father Short.

FATHER SHORT came down the lane,
Oh, I'm obliged to hammer and smite
From four in the morning till eight at night,
For a bad master, and a worse dame.

I had a Little Husband.

I HAD a little husband,
  No bigger than my thumb;
I put him in a pint pot,
  And there I bid him drum.

I bought a little horse,
  That galloped up and down;
I bridled him, and saddled him,
  And sent him out of town.

I gave him some garters,
  To garter up his nose,
And a little handkerchief
  To wipe his pretty nose.

Higgledy, Piggledy, here We Lie.

HIGGLEDY, piggledy,
    Here we lie,
  Picked and plucked,
    And put in a pie.
My first is snapping, snarling, growling,
My second's industrious, romping, and prowling.
    Higgledy, piggledy,
      Here we lie,
    Picked and plucked,
      And put in a pie.
        (*Currants.*)

HERE we come gathering
                nuts and may,
Nuts and may, nuts and may,
Here we come gathering
                nuts and may,
On a cold and frosty morning.

As I was going to St. Ives

AS I was going to St. Ives,
I met a man with seven wives,
Every wife had seven sacks,
Every sack had seven cats,
Every cat had seven kits—
Kits, cats, sacks, and wives,
How many were there going to St. Ives?

(*One.*)

Merry are the Bells.

MERRY are the bells, and merry would they ring,
Merry was myself, and merry could I sing;
With a merry ding-dong, happy, gay, and free,
And a merry sing-song, happy let us be!

Waddle goes your gait, and hollow are your hose,
Noddle goes your pate, and purple is your nose;
Merry is your sing-song, happy, gay, and free,
With a merry ding-dong, happy let us be!

Merry have we met, and merry have we been,
Merry let us part, and merry meet again;
With our merry sing-song, happy, gay, and free,
And a merry ding-dong, happy let us be!

A Frog He Would a-Wooing Go.

A FROG he would a-wooing go,
     Sing heigho, says Rowley,
Wether his mother would let him or no;
With a rowley, powley, gammon. and spinach,
     Heigho, says Anthony Rowley,

So off he marches with his opera hat,
     Heigho, says Rowley,
And on the way he met with a rat,
     With a rowley, powley etc.

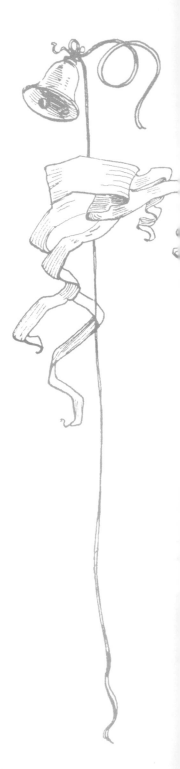

And when they came to Mouse's Hall,
  Heigho, says Rowley,
They gave a loud knock, and they gave a loud call,
  With a rowley, powley, etc.

"Pray, Mrs. Mouse, are you within?"
    Heigho, says Rowley;
"Yes, kind sir, I am sitting to spin,"
    With a rowley, powley, etc.

"Pray, Mrs. Mouse, will you give us some beer?"
    Heigho, says Rowley;
"For froggy and I are fond of good cheer,"
    With a rowley, powley, etc.

Now while they all were a merry-making,
    Heigho, says Rowley,
The cat and her kittens came tumbling in,
    With a rowley, powley, etc.

The cat she seized the rat by the crown,
      Heigho, says Rowley;
The kittens they pulled the little mouse down,
      With a rowley, powley, etc.

This put poor frog in a terrible fright,
      Heigho, says Rowley,
So he took up his hat and wished them good-night,
      With a rowley, powley, etc.

But as Froggy was crossing over a brook,
      Heigho, says Rowley,
A lily-white duck came and gobbled him up,
      With a rowley, powley, etc.

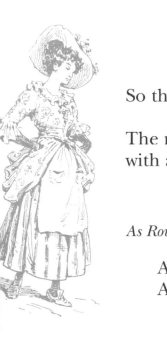

So there was an end of one, two, and three,
      Heigho, says Rowley,
The rat, the mouse, and the little Frog-ee!
with a rowley, powley, gammon, and spinach,
      Heigho, says Anthony Rowley.

As Round as an Apple.

    As round as an apple, as deep as a cup,
    And all the king's horses can't pull it up.
                       (*A Well.*)

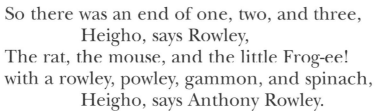

"If all the seas were one sea."

If All the Seas were One Sea.

IF all the seas were one sea,
What a *great* sea that would be!
And if all the trees were one tree,
What a *great* tree that would be!
And if all the axes were one axe,
What a *great* axe that would be !

And if all the men were one man,
What a *great* man he would be!
And if the *great* man took the *great* axe,
And cut down the *great* tree,
And let it fall into the *great* sea,
What a splish splash *that* would be!

The Dove Says, "Coo, coo."

THE dove says, "Coo, coo, what shall I do"?
I can scarce maintain two."
"Pooh! pooh! "Says the wren; "I have got ten,
And I keep them all like gentlemen."

A Little Pig Found

A LITTLE Pig found a fifty-dollar note,
And purchased a hat and a very fine coat,
    With trousers, and stockings, and shoes;
Cravat, and shirt-collar, and gold-headed cane;
Then, proud as could be, did he march up the lane;
    Says he, "I shall hear all the news."

Up Hill and Down Dale.

UP hill and down dale;
Butter is made in every vale;
And if that Nancy Cook
Is a good girl,
She shall have a spouse,
And make butter anon,
Before her old grandmother
Grows a young man.

How many miles to Babylon?

OW many miles is it to Babylon?—
Threescore miles and ten.
Can I get there by candle-light?—
Yes, and back again!
If your heels are nimble and light,
You may get there by candle-light.

There was a Little Green House.

THERE was a Little Green House,
And in the little green house
There was a little brown house,
And in the little brown house
There was a little yellow house,
And in the little yellow house
There was a little white house,
And in the little white house
There was a little heart.

(*A walnut.*)

See-saw, Margery Daw.

SEE-SAW Margery Daw,
Jenny shall have a new master:
She shall have but a penny a day,
Because she can't work any faster.

Whistle, Daughter, Whistle.

WHISTLE, daughter, whistle, daughter dear.
I cannot whistle, mammy, I cannot whistle clear.
Whistle, daughter, whistle, whistle for a pound.
I cannot whistle, mammy, I cannot make a sound.

Bat, Bat, Come under My Hat.

> BAT, bat,
> Come under my hat,
> And I'll give you a slice of bacon;
> And when I bake
> I'll give you a cake,
> If I am not mistaken.

Monday's Child.

> MONDAY'S child is fair of face,
> Tuesday's child is full of grace,
> Wednesday's child is full of woe,
> Thursday's child has far to go,
> Friday's child is loving and giving,
> Saturday's child works hard for its living;
> And a child that is born on Christmas Day
> Is fair, and wise, and good, and gay.

If All the World.

> IF all the world was apple-pie,
> And all the sea was ink,
> And all the trees were bread and cheese,
> What should we have for drink?

Multiplication is Vexation.

> MULTIPLICATION is vexation,
> Division is just as bad;
> The rule of Three perplexes me,
> And Practice drives me mad.

Multiplication is Vexation.

Humpty Dumpty.

HUMPTY DUMPTY sat on a wall,
Humpty Dumpty had a great fall;
Threescore men and threescore more
Cannot place Humpty Dumpty as he was before.

Hot Cross Buns!

HOT-cross buns!
Hot-cross buns!
One a penny, two a penny,
Hot-cross buns!

Hot-cross buns!
Hot-cross buns!
If ye have no daughters,
Give them to your sons.

Did You See My Wife?

ID you see my wife, did you see, did you see,
    Did you see my wife looking for me?
She wears a straw bonnet, with white ribbons on it,
    And dimity petticoats over her knee.

Birds of a Feather.

    BIRDS of a feather flock together,
        And so will pigs and swine;
    Rats and mice will have their choice,
        And so will I have mine.

Wooley Foster has Gone to Sea.

    WOOLEY FOSTER has gone to sea,
    With silver buckles at his knee;
    When he comes back he'll marry me,
        Bonny Wooley Foster

    Wooley Foster has a cow,
    Black and white about the mow;
    Open the gates and let her through,
        Wooley Foster's ain cow!

    Wooley Foster has a hen,
    Cockle button, cockle ben,
    She lays eggs for gentlemen,
        But none for Wooley Foster.

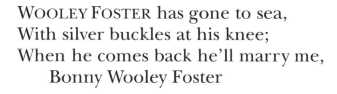

A Dillar, a Dollar.

A DILLAR, a dollar,
A ten o'clock scholar,
What makes you come so soon?
You used to come at ten o'clock,
And now you come at noon.

Awa', Birds, Away!

AWA', birds, away !
Take a little, leave a little,
And do not come again;
For if you do,
I will shoot you through,
And there is an end of you.

Charley, Charley!

CHARLEY, Charley, stole the barley
    Out of the baker's shop;
The baker came out, and gave him a clout,
    And made poor Charley hop.

Jeannie Come Tie my Bonnie Cravat.

JEANNIE, come tie my,
Jeannie, come tie my,
Jeannie, come tie my bonnie cravat;
I've tied it behind,
I've tied it before,
And I've tied it so often, I'll tie it no more.

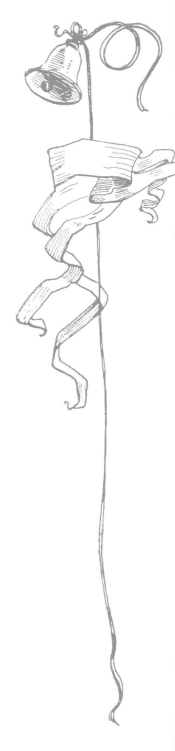

"What makes you come so soon?"

TOM, Tom, the piper's son.

TOM, Tom the piper's son,
He learned to play when he was young;
But all the tunes that he could play
Was "Over the hills and far away,"
    Over the hills, and a great way off,
    And the will blow my top-knot off.

NOW, Tom with his pipe made such a noise,
That he pleased both the girls and boys,
And they stopped to hear him play,
"Over the hills and far away."

Tom with his pipe did play with such skill
That those who heard him could never keep still:
Whenever they heard they began for to dance,—
Even pigs on their hind legs
        would after him prance.

As Dolly was milking her cow one day,
Tom took out his pipe and began for to play;
So Doll and the cow danced "the Cheshire round,"
Till the pail was broke,
        and the milk ran on the ground.

He met old Dame Trot with a basket of eggs,
He used his pipe and she used her legs;
She danced about till the eggs were all broke,
She began for to fret, but he laughed at the joke.

He saw a cross fellow was beating an ass,
Heavy laden with pots, pans, dishes, and glass;
He took out his pipe and played them a tune,
And the jackass's load was lightened full soon.

As I Was Going Along.

As I was going along, long, long,
A-singing a comical song, song, song,
The lane that I went was so long, long, long,
And the song that I sung was as long, long, long,
And so I went singing along.

I Would if I Could.

I WOULD if I could,
If I couldn't how could I?
I couldn't without I could, could I?
Could you, without you could, could ye?
Could ye, could ye?
Could you, without you could, could ye?

Lavender Blue and Rosemary Green.

LAVENDER blue and Rosemary green,
When I am king you shall be queen;
Call up my maids at four of the clock,
Some to the wheel, and some to the rock,
Some to make hay, and some to thresh corn,
And you and I will keep the bed warm.

I Went to the Wood.

I WENT to the wood and got it;
I sat me down and looked at it;
The more I looked at it the less I liked it,
And I brought it home because I couldn't help it.

(A thorn.)

l Had a Little Cow.

> I HAD a little cow;
> Hey-diddle, ho-diddle !
> I had a little cow, and it had a little calf;
> Hey-diddle, ho-diddle; and there's my song half.
>
> I had a little cow;
> Hey-diddle, ho-diddle !
> I had a little cow, and I drove it to the stall;
> Hey diddle, ho-diddle; and there's my song all !

Little Cock Robin.

> LITTLE Cock Robin peeped out of his cabin
> To see the cold winter come in.
> Tit for tat, what matter for that ?—
> He'll hide his head under his wing !

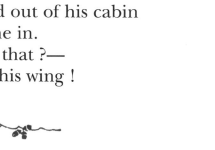

Mary had a Little Lamb

MARY had a little lamb,
  Its fleece was white as snow;
  And everywhere that Mary went,
The lamb was sure to go.

He followed her to school one day;
  That was against the rule;
It made the children laugh and play
  To see a lamb at school.

And so the teacher turned him out,
  But still he lingered near,
And waited patiently about
  Till Mary did appear.

Mary had a Little Lamb

Then he ran to her, and laid
 His head upon her arm,
As if he said, "I'm not afraid—
 You'll keep me from all harm."

"What makes the lamb love Mary so?
 The eager children cry.
"Oh, Mary loves the lamb, you know,"
 The teacher did reply.

And you each gentle animal
 In confidence may bind,
And make them follow at your will,
 If you are only kind.

Here am I.

HERE am I,
Little jumping Joan.
When nobody's with me,
I'm always alone.

Hurly, Burly.

HURLY, burly, trumpet trase,
The cow was in the market-place.
Some goes far, and some goes near,
But whcrc shall this poor hcnchman steer?

I Went up One Pair of Stairs.

1. I WENT UP one pair of stairs.
2. Just like me.
1. I went up two pair of stairs.
2. Just likc mc.
1. I went into a room.
2. Just like me.
1. I looked out of a window.
2. Just like me.
1. And there I saw a monkey.
2. Just like me.

Elsie Marley.

ELSIE MARLEY has grown so fine
She won't get up to feed the swine;
She lies in bed till half-past nine—
Ay! truly she doth take her time.

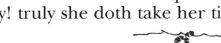

Poor Dog Bright.

POOR Dog Bright
Ran off with all his might,
Because the cat was after him—
Poor Dog Bright !

Poor Cat Fright
Ran off with all her might,
Because the dog was after her—
Poor Cat Fright !

Johnny Shall Have A New Bonnet.

JOHNNY shall have a new bonnet,
  And Johnny shall go to the fair,
And Johnny shall have a blue ribbon
  To tie up his bonny brown hair.

And why may not I love Johnny?
  And why may not Johnny love me?
And why may not I love Johnny
  As well as another body?

And here's a leg for a stocking,
  And here's a leg, for a shoe;
And he has a kiss for his daddy,
  And two for his mammy, I trow.

And why may not I love Johnny?
  And why may not Johnny love me?
And why may not I love Johnny
As well as another body?

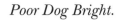

A Cat Came Fiddling Out of a Barn.

A CAT came fiddling out of a barn,
  With a pair of bag-pipes under her arm;
  She could sing nothing but fiddle-de-dee,
  The mouse has married the humble-bee;
Pipe, cat—dance, mouse—
We'll have a wedding at our good house.

I'll Sing you a Song,
    though Not Very Long.

I'LL sing you a song,
  Though not very long,
      Yet I think it's
        as pretty as any;
      Put your hand
          in your purse,
        You'll never be worse,
      And give the
        poor singer
            a penny.

PUSSY-CAT
Pussy-cat,
where have you been?

"I've been
up to London
to look at the Queen."

Pussy-cat, pussy-cat,
what did you there?
"I frightened
a little mouse
under the chair."

I HAD a little hen,
the prettiest ever seen.

I Had a Little Hen.

I HAD a little hen, the prettiest ever seen;
She washed me the dishes, and kept the house clean;
She went to the mill to fetch me some flour,
She brought it home in less than an hour;
She baked me my bread, she brewed me my ale,
She sat by the fire and told many a fine tale.

Marble Walls.

IN marble walls as white as milk,
Lined with a skin as soft as silk,
Within a fountain crystal clear,
A golden apple doth appear.
No doors there are to this stronghold,
Yet thieves break in and steal the gold.   (*An egg.*)

A man of Words.

A MAN of words and not of deeds
Is like a garden full of weeds;
For when the weeds begin to grow,
Then doth the garden overflow.

Hey Diddle, Dinketty.

HEY diddle, dinketty, pompetty, pet,
The merchants of London they wear scarlet;
Silk in the collar, and gold in the hem,
So merrily march the merchantmen.

I Saw Three Ships

I SAW three ships come sailing by,
    Come sailing by, come sailing by;
I saw three ships come sailing by,
    New Year's Day in the morning.

And what do you think was in them then?
    Was in them then, was in them then?
And what do you think was in them then?
    New Year's Day in the morning.

Three pretty girls were in them then,
    Were in them then, were in them then,
Three pretty girls were in them then,
    New Year's Day in the morning.

One could whistle, and another could sing,
    And the other could play on the violin—
Such joy was there at my wedding,
    New Year's Day in the morning.

As I Went Through the Garden Gap.

As I went through the garden gap!
Who should I meet but Dick Red-cap!
A stick in his hand, a stone in his throat.
If you'll tell me this riddle, I'll give you a groat.
                    (*A cherry.*)

Jack and Jill.

Jack and Jill went up the hill,
To fetch a pail of water;
Jack fell down, and broke his crown,
And Jill came tumbling after.

Dame, Get Up, and Bake Your Pies.

DAME, get up and bake your pies,
Bake your pies, bake your pies,
Dame, get up and bake your pies,
On Christmas-day in the morning

Dame, what makes your maidens lie,
Maidens lie, maidens lie;
Dame, what makes your maidens lie,
On Christmas-day in the morning?

Dame, what makes your ducks to die,
Ducks to die, ducks to die;
Dame, what makes your ducks to die,
On Christmas-day in the morning?

Their wings are cut, and they cannot fly,
Cannot fly, cannot fly;
Their wings are cut, and they cannot fly,
On Christmas-day in the morning.

*The Old Woman Who Rode
on a Broom.*

THERE was an old woman who rode on a broom,
   With a high gee ho, gee humble;
     And she took her old cat behind for a groom,
   With a bimble, bamble, bumble.

They travelled along till they came to the sky,
   With a high gee ho, gee humble;
But the journey so long made them very hungry,
   With a bimble, bamble, bumble.

Says Tom, "I can find nothing here to eat,
    with a high gee ho, gee humble;
So let us go back again, I entreat,
    with a bimble, bamble, bumble."

The old woman would not go back so soon,
    with a high gee ho, gee humble;
For she wanted to visit the man in the moon,
    with a bimble, bamble, bumble.

Says Tom, "I'll go back myself to our house,
    With a high gee ho, gee humble;
For there I can catch a good rat or a mouse,
    with a bimble, bamble, bumble."

"But," says the old woman, "how will you go?
 With a high gee ho, gee humble;
You shan't have my nag, I protest and vow,
 With a bimble, bamble, bumble."

"No, no," says Tom, "I've a plan of my own,
 With a high gee ho, gee humble;"
So he slid down the rainbow,
 With a bimble, bamble, bumble.

So now, if you happen to visit the sky,
 With a high gee ho, gee humble,
And want to come back, you Tom's method may try,
 with a bimble, bamble, bumble.

Feeding the Chicks.

Cock a Doodle Doo!

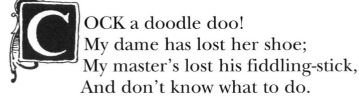

COCK a doodle doo!
My dame has lost her shoe;
My master's lost his fiddling-stick,
And don't know what to do.

Cock a doodle doo!
What is my dame to do?
Till master finds his fiddling-stick,
She'll dance without her shoe.

Cock a doodle doo !
My dame has lost her shoe,
And master's found his fiddling-stick,
Sing doodle doodle doo!

Cock a doodle doo,
My dame will dance with you,
While master fiddles his fiddling-stick,
For dame and doodle doo.

Cock a doodle doo!
Dame has lost her shoe;
Gone to bed and scratched her head,
And can't tell what to do.

Cock Crows in the Morn.

COCK crows in the morn,
  To tell us to rise,
And he who lies late
will never be wise:

For early to bed,
  And early to rise,
Is the way to be healthy
  And wealthy and wise.

Little Bob Robin.

LITTLE Bob Robin, where do you live?
Up in yon wood, sir, on a hazel twig.

The Old Man Who Lived in a Wood.

THERE was an old man who lived in a wood,
　　As you may plainly see;
He said he could do as much work in a day
　　As his wife could do in three.
"With all my heart," the old woman said;
　　"If that you will allow,
To-morrow you'll stay at home in my stead,
　　And I'll go drive the plough."

"But you must milk the Tidy cow,
　　For fear that she go dry;
And you must feed the little pigs
　　That are within the sty;
And you must mind the speckled hen,
　　For fear she lay away;
And you must reel the spool of yarn
　　That I spun yesterday."

High! Tidy l ho! Tidy! high!
　　Tidy, do stand still!
If ever I milk you, Tidy, again,
　　'Twill be sore against my will."
He went to feed the little pigs,
　　That were within the sty;
He hit his head against the beam,
　　And he made the blood to fly.

He went to mind the speckled hen,
For fear she'd lay astray,
    And he forgot the spool of yarn
His wife spun yesterday.
    So he swore by the sun, the moon, and the stars,
And the green leaves on the tree,
    If his wife didn't do a day's work in her life.
She should never be ruled by he.

Dance, Little Baby.

DANCE, little baby, dance up high,
Never mind, baby, mother is by;
Crow and caper, caper and crow,
There, little baby, there you go;

Up to the ceiling, down to the ground,
Backwards and forwards, round and round;
Dance, little baby, and mother will sing,
with the merry coral, ding, ding, ding!

Flour of England.

FLOUR of England, fruit of Spain,
Met together in a shower of rain;
Put in a bag tied round with a string,
If you'll tell me this riddle, I'll give you a ring.
                    (*A plum pudding*)

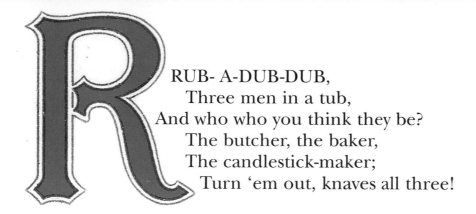

RUB- A-DUB-DUB,
Three men in a tub,
And who who you think they be?
The butcher, the baker,
The candlestick-maker;
Turn 'em out, knaves all three!

Moss Was a Little Man.

Moss was a little man, and a little mare did buy;
For kicking and for sprawling, none her could come nigh;
She could trot, she could amble,
          and could canter here and there,
But one night she strayed away—so Moss lost his mare.

Moss got up next morning to catch her fast asleep,
And round about the frosty fields so nimbly he did creep.
Dead in a ditch he found her,
          and glad to find her there;
So I'll tell you by-and-by how Moss caught his mare.

"Rise! stupid, rise!" he thus to her did say;
"Arise, you beast, you drowsy beast,
          get up without delay,

For I must ride you to the town,
so don't lie sleeping there; he put the halter round
          her neck— so Moss caught his mare.

Old Mistress McShuttle.

    OLD Mistress McShuttle
    Lived in a coal-scuttle,
    Along with her dog and her cat:
    What they ate I can't tell,
    But 'tis known very well
    That none of the party were fat.

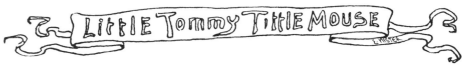

LITTLE TOMMY Tittlemouse
Lived in a little house;
He caught fishes
In other men's ditches.

Up at Piccadilly, Oh!

UP at Piccadilly, oh !
    The coachman takes his stand,
And when he meets a pretty girl,
    He takes her by the hand.
Whip away for ever, oh!
    Drive away so clever, oh!
All the way to Bristol, oh!
    He drives her four-in-hand.

Joey Was A bad man.

JOEY was a bad man, Joey was a thief;
Joey came to my house and stole a piece of beef;

I went to Joey's house, Joey was not at home;
Joey came to my house and stole a marrow-bone.

I went to Joey's house, Joey was asleep,
I took the marrow-bone, and beat about his feet.

There was a Fat Man of Bombay.

THERE was a fat man of Bombay,
Who was smoking one sunshiny day,
   When a bird, called a snipe,
   Flew away with his pipe,
Which vexed the fat man of Bombay.

Sing a Song of Sixpence.

SING a song of sixpence,
   A pocket full of rye;
Four and twenty blackbirds
   Baked in a pie;

When the pie was opened,
   The birds began to sing;
Was not that a dainty dish
   To set before the king?

   The king was in the parlour,
   Counting out his money;
The queen was in the kitchen,
   Eating bread and honey;

The maid was in the garden,
   Hanging out the clothes;
There came a little blackbird,
   And snipped off her nose.

THE Queen of Hearts,
She made
some tarts,
All on a
summer's day,
The knave of hearts,
He stole some tarts,
And took them clean away.

WHERE are you going,
my pretty maid?
"I'm going a milking,
sir," she said.

SING a song of sixpence,
A pocket full of rye;
Four-and-twenty blackbirds
Baked in a pie.

What is the Rhyme for Porringer?

WHAT is the rhyme for *porringer?*
The king he had a daughter fair,
And gave the Prince of Orange her.

The Queen of Hearts.

THE queen of hearts
    She made some tarts,
All on a summer's day;
    The knave of hearts
    He stole those tarts,
And with them ran away.

The king of hearts
    Called for those tarts,
And beat the knave full sore;
    The knave of hearts
    Brought back those tarts,
And said he'd ne'er steal more.

Where Are You Going, My Pretty Maid?

"WHERE are you going, my pretty maid?"
"I'm going a-milking, sir," she said.

"May I go with you, my pretty maid?"
"You're kindly welcome, sir," she said.

"What is your father, my pretty maid?"
"My father's a farmer, sir," she said.

"What is your fortune, my pretty maid?"
"My face is my fortune, sir," she said.

"Then I can't marry you, my pretty maid!"
"Nobody asked you, sir!" she said.

Here We Go Up, Up, Up.

HERE we go up, up, up,
  And here we go down, down, downy,
And here we go backwards and forwards,
  And here we go round, round, roundy.

Oh, Dear What Can the Matter Be?

OH, dear! what can the matter be?
Two old women got up an apple-tree;
One came down,
And the other stayed till Saturday.

For Every Evil Under the Sun.

FOR every evil under the sun,
There is a remedy, or there is none.
If there be one, try and find it,
If there be none, never mind it.

PLEASE to remember
The Fifth of November,
Gunpowder, treason, and plot;
I know no reason
Why gunpowder treason
Should ever be forgot.

See, Saw, Sacradown.

SEE, saw, sacradown,
Which is the way to London town?
One foot up, the other foot down,
And that is the way to London town.

Little Boy Blue.

LITTLE Boy Blue, come blow up your horn,
The sheep's in the meadow, the cow's in the corn;

Where's the little boy that tends the sheep?
He's under the haycock, fast asleep.

Go wake him, go wake him. Oh! no, not I;
For if I awake him, he'll certainly cry.

Once I Saw a little Bird.

ONCE I saw a little bird
    Come hop, hop, hop;
So I cried, "Little bird,
    Will you stop, stop, stop?"
And was going to the window
    To say, "How do you do?"
But he shook his little tail,
    And far away he flew.

SEE, see! what shall I see?
A horse's head where his tail should be!

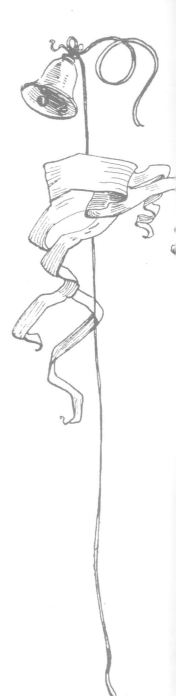

The Marriage of Cock Robin
and Jenny Wren.

IT was on a merry time,
  When Jenny Wren was young,
So neatly as she danced,
  And so sweetly as she sung,—

Robin Redbreast lost his heart:
  He was a gallant bird;
He doffed his hat to Jenny,
  And thus to her he said:

"My dearest Jenny Wren,
  If you will but be mine,
You shall dine on cherry-pie,
  And drink nice currant-wine.

  "I'll dress you like a Goldfinch,
Or like a Peacock gay;
So if you'll have me, Jenny,
Let us appoint the day."

Jenny blushed behind her fan,
  And thus declared her mind:
"Then let it be to-morrow, Bob;
  I take your offer kind.

"Cherry-pie is very good;
  So is currant-wine;
But I will wear my brown gown,
  And never dress too fine."

Robin rose up early,
  At the break of day;
He flew to Jenny Wren's house,
  To sing a roundelay.

He met the Cock and Hen,
  And bade the Cock declare,
This was his wedding-day
  With Jenny wren the fair.

The Cock then blew his horn,
  To let the neighbours know
This was Robin's wedding-day,
  And they might see the show.

And first came Parson Rook,
  With his spectacles and band;
And one of Mother Hubbard's books
  He held within his hand.

Then followed him the Lark,
  For he could sweetly sing;
And he was to be clerk
  At Cock Robin's wedding.

He sang of Robin's love
  For little Jenny Wren;
And when he came unto the end,
  Then he began again.

The Goldfinch came on next,
  To give away the bride;
The Linnet, being bridesmaid,
  Walked by Jenny's side.

And as she was a walking,
  Said, "Upon my word,
I think that your Cock Robin
  Is a very pretty bird."

The Blackbird and the Thrush,
  And charming Nightingale;
whose sweet "jug" sweetly echoes
  Through every grove and dale;

The Sparrow and Tomtit,
  And many more were there;
All came to see the wedding
  Of Jenny Wren the fair.

The Marriage.

The Bullfinch walked by Robin,
  And thus to him did say:
"Pray, mark, friend Robin Redbreast,
  That Goldfinch dressed so gay;

"What though her gay apparel
  Becomes her very well;
Yet Jenny's modest dress and look
  Must bear away the bell!"

Then came the bride and bridegroom;
  Quite plainly was she dressed;
And blushed so much, her cheeks were
  As red as Robin's breast.

But Robin cheered her up;
  "My pretty Jen," said he,
"We're going to be married,
  And happy we shall be."

"Oh, then," says Parson Rook,
  "Who gives this maid away?"
"I do," says the Goldfinch,
  "And her fortune I will pay;

"Here's a bag of grain of many sorts,
  And other things beside;
Now happy be the bridegroom,
  And happy be the bride!"

"And will you have her, Robin
  To be your wedded wife?"
"Yes, I will," says Robin,
  "And love her all my life."

"And you will have him, Jenny,
  Your husband now to be?"
"Yes, I will," says Jenny,
  "And love him heartily."

Then on her finger fair,
  Cock Robin put the ring;
"You're married now," says Parson Rook;
  while the Lark aloud did sing:

"Happy be the bridegroom,
  And happy be the bride!
And may not man, nor bird, nor beast,
  This happy pair divide."

The birds were asked to dine;
  Not Jenny's friends alone,
But every pretty songster
  That had Cock Robin known.

They had a cherry-pie,
  Besides some currant-wine,
And every guest brought something,
That sumptuous they might dine.

The Wedding Breakfast..

Now they all sat or stood,
  To eat and to drink;
And every one said what
  He happened to think.

They each took a bumper,
  And drank to the pair;
Cock Robin the bridegroom,
  And Jenny Wren the fair.

The dinner things removed,
  They all began to sing;
And soon they made the place
  Near a mile around to ring.

The concert it was fine;
  And every bird tried
Who best should sing for Robin,
  And Jenny Wren the bride,

When in came the Cuckoo,
  And made a great rout;
He caught hold of Jenny,
  And pulled her about.

Cock Robin was angry,
  And so was the Sparrow,
Who fetched in a hurry
  His bow and his arrow.

  His aim then he took,
But he took it not right;
His skill was not good,
  Or he shot in a fright;

For the Cuckoo he missed,
  But Cock Robin he killed!—
And all the birds mourned
  That his blood was so spilled

The Death of Cock Robin.

The Death and Burial of Cock Robin.

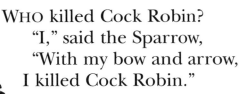

WHO killed Cock Robin?
  "I," said the Sparrow,
  "With my bow and arrow,
I killed Cock Robin."

  This is the Sparrow,
With his bow and arrow.

  Who saw him die?
"I," said the Fly,
  "With my little eye,
And I saw him die."

This is the little Fly,
Who saw Cock Robin die.

  Who caught his blood?
  "I," said the Fish,
  "With my little dish,
  And I caught his blood."

  This is the Fish
That held the dish.

Who made his shroud?
  "I," said the Beetle,
  "With my little needle,
And I made his shroud."

This is the Beetle,
With his thread and needle.

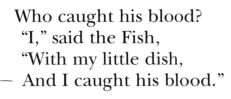

Who shall dig his grave?
  "I," said the Owl,
  "With my spade and show'l,
And I'll dig his grave."

This is the Owl,
  With his spade and show'l.

Who'll be the parson?
  "I," said the Rook,
  "With my little book,
And I'll be the parson."

This is the Rook,
      Reading the book.

          Who'll be the clerk?
            "I," said the Lark,
            "If it's not in the dark,
          And I'll be the clerk."

This is the clerk,
Saying "Amen" like a clerk.

"Who'll carry him to the grave?
  "I," said the Kite,
  "If 'tis not in the night,
And I'll carry him to his grave."

This is the Kite,
About to take flight.

Who'll carry the link?
"I," said the Linnet,
    "I'll fetch it in a minute,
And I'll carry the link."

This is the Linnet,
And a link with fire in it.

Who'll be the chief mourner?
 "I," said the Dove,
 "I mourn for my love,
And I'll be chief mourner."

This is the Dove,
Who Cock Robin did love.

 Who'll sing a psalm?
"I," said the Thrush,
    As she sat in a bush,
 "And I'll sing a psalm."

 This is the Thrush,
Singing psalms from a bush.

 And who'll toll the bell?
"I," said the Bull,
 "Because I can
pull;"
And so, Cock
Robin,
    farewell.

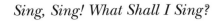

Sing, Sing! What Shall I Sing?

SING, sing! what shall I sing?
The cat has eat the pudding-string !
Do, do! what shall I do?
The cat has bit it quite in two.

Pease-pudding Hot.

PEASE-PUDDING hot,
    Pease-pudding cold,
Pease-pudding in the pot,
    Nine days old.

Some like it hot,
    Some like it cold,
Some like it in the pot,
    Nine days old.

Peter, Peter, Pumpkin-eater.

PETER, Peter, pumpkin-eater,
Had a wife, and couldn't keep her;
He put her in a pumpkin-shell,
And there he kept her very well.

Peter, Peter, pumpkin-eater,
Had another and didn't love her;
Peter learned to read and spell,
And then he loved her very well.

HEY! diddle, diddle,

The cat and the fiddle,

The cow jumped

over the moon;

The little dog laughed

to see such sport,

And the dish ran away

with the spoon.

As I Was Going o'er Westminster Bridge.

As I was going o'er Westminster Bridge,
I met with a Westminster scholar;
He pulled off his cap an' drew off his glove,
And wished me a very good morrow.
    What is his name?

Margery Mutton-pie.

MARGERY MUTTON-PIE and Johnny Bo-peep,
They met together in Gracechurch-street;
In and out, in and out, over the way,
Oh! says Johnny, 'tis chop-nose day.

Simple Simon Met a Pie-man.

SIMPLE Simon met a pieman
  Going to the fair;
Says Simple Simon to the pieman,
  "Let me taste your ware."

Says the pieman to Simple Simon,
  "Show me first your penny;"
Says Simple Simon to the pieman,
  "Indeed I have not any."

Simple Simon went a-fishing
  For to catch a whale;

All the water he had got
 Was in his mother's pail.

Simple Simon went to look
 If plums grew on a thistle;
He pricked his fingers very much,
 Which made poor Simon whistle.

THERE was a little girl
    Who wore a little hood,
And a curl down the middle
    of her forehead;
when she was good,
    She was very, very good,
But when she was bad,
      she was horrid.

CURLY locks! curly locks!
    Wilt thou be mine?
Thou shalt not wash dishes,
    Nor yet feed the swine;
But sit on a cushion
    And sew a fine seam,
And feed upon strawberries,
    sugar, and cream!

Over the Water.

OVER the water and over the lea,
And over the water to Charley.
Charley loves good ale and wine,
And Charley loves good brandy,
And Charley loves a pretty girl,
As sweet as sugar-candy.

Over the water and over the sea,
And over the water to Charley.
I'll have none of your nasty beef,
Nor I'll have none of your barley;
But I'll have some of your very best flour,
To make a white cake for my Charley.

Pussy-cat Ate the Dumplings.

PUSSY-CAT ate the dumplings, the dumplings,
Pussy-cat ate the dumplings.
    Mamma stood by,
    And cried, "Oh, fie!
Why did you eat the dumplings ?"

The Girl in the Lane.

THE girl in the lane, that couldn't speak plain,
    Cried, "Gobble, gobble, gobble";
The man on the hill, that couldn't stand still,
    Went hobble hobble hobble.

Little Betty Blue.

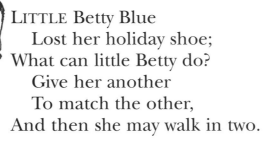

LITTLE Betty Blue
   Lost her holiday shoe;
What can little Betty do?
   Give her another
   To match the other,
And then she may walk in two.

1, 2, 3, 4, 5.

1, 2, 3, 4, 5!
   I caught a hare alive;
6, 7, 8, 9, 10!
   I let her go again.

London Bridge is Broken Down.

LONDON Bridge is broken down,
    Dance o'er my lady Lee;
London Bridge is broken down,
    With a gay lady.

How shall we build it up again?
    Dance o'er my lady Lee;
How shall we build it up again'
    With a gay lady.

Silver and gold will be stole away,
    Dance o'er my lady Lee;
Silver and gold will be stole away,
    With a gay lady.

Build it up again with iron and steel,
    Dance o'er my lady Lee;
Build it up with iron and steel,
    With a gay lady.

Iron and steel will bend and bow,
    Dance o'er my lady Lee;
Iron and steel will bend and bow,
    With a gay lady.

Build it up with wood and clay,
    Dance o'er my lady Lee:
Build it up with wood and clay,
    With a gay lady.

Wood and clay will wash away,
    Dance o'er my lady Lee;
Wood and clay will wash away,
    With a gay lady.

Build it up with stone so strong,
    Dance o'er my lady Lee;
Huzza! 'twill last for ages long,
    With a gay lady.

See a Pin and Pick it Up.

SEE a pin and pick it up,
All the day you'll have good luck;
See a pin and let it lay,
Bad luck you'll have all the day!

Pussy-Cat, Wussy Cat.

PUSSY CAT, wussy-cat, with a white foot,
When is your wedding? for I'll come to't.
The beer's to brew, the bread's to bake,
Pussy-cat, pussy-cat, don't be too late.

The Man in the Wilderness.

THE man in the wilderness asked me,
How many strawberries grew in the sea.
I answered him, as I thought good,
As many red herrings as grow in the wood

DOCTOR FOSTER went to Gloucester,

In a shower of rain;

He stepped into a puddle up to his middle,

And never went there again.

There Was a King.

THERE was a king met a king
    In a narrow lane;
Says this king to that king,
    "Where have you been?"

Oh I I've been a-hunting
    With my dog and my doe.
"Pray lend him to me,
    That I may do so."

There's the dog—take the dog.
    "What's the dog's name?"
"I've told you already"
"Pray tell me again."

The King of France.

THE King of France went up the hill,
    With twenty thousand men;
The King of France came down the hill,
    And ne'er went up again.

My Little Old Man.

MY little old man and I fell out
I'll tell you what 'twas all about;
I had money and he had none,
And that's the way the row begun.

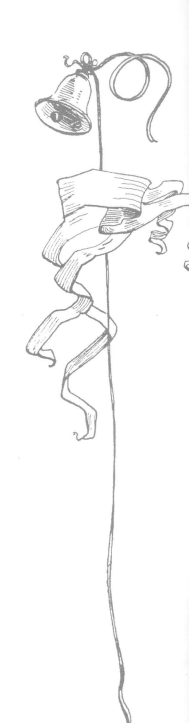

Tommy Kept a Chandler's Shop.

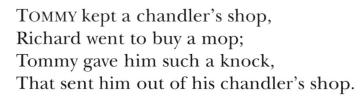

TOMMY kept a chandler's shop,
Richard went to buy a mop;
Tommy gave him such a knock,
That sent him out of his chandler's shop.

Bow, wow, wow,
whose dog art thou?
Little Tom Tinker's dog,
Bow, wow, wow.

I HAD a little pony,
    His name was Dapple-gray;
I lent him to a lady,
    To ride a mile away;

She whipped him, she slashed him,
    She rode him through
    the mire;
I would not lend
my pony now
For all the
lady's hire.

The Lion and the Unicorn.

THE lion and the unicorn
 Were fighting for the crown;
The lion beat the unicorn
 All round about the town.

Some gave them white bread,
 And some gave them brown;
Some gave them plum-cake,
 And sent them out of town.

Dance to Your Daddy.

DANCE- to your daddy,
My little babby;
Dance to your daddy,
My little lamb.

You shall have a fishy,
In a little dishy;
You shall have a fishy
when the boat comes in.

Riddle Me. Riddle Me, Ree.

RIDDLE me, riddle me, ree,
A hawk sat upon a tree;
And he says to himself, says he,
"Oh dear! what a fine bird I be!"

One Misty, Moisty Morning.

ONE misty, moisty morning,
    When cloudy was the weather,
I chanced to meet an old man
    Clothed all in leather;
He began to compliment,
    And I began to grin,—
"How do you do," and "How do you do,"
    And "How do you do" again!

Robert Rowley.

ROBERT ROWLEY rolled a round roll round,
A round roll Robert Rowley rolled round;
Where rolled the round roll Robert Rowley rolled round?

Robin and Richard.

ROBIN and Richard were two pretty men;
They laid in bed till- the clock struck ten;
Then up starts- Robin, and looks at the sky:
"Oho! brother Richard, the sun's very high."

Old Mother Twitchett.

OLD Mother Twitchett had but one eye,
And a long tail which she let fly;
And every time she went over a gap,
She left a bit of her tail in a trap.
                (*A needle and thread.*)

There Was an Old Woman.

THERE was an old woman lived under a hill:
And if she's not gone, she lives there still.

Solomon Grundy.

SOLOMON GRUNDY,
Born on a Monday,
Christened on Tuesday,
Married on Wednesday,
Took ill on Thursday,
Worse on Friday,
Died on Saturday,
Buried on Sunday:
This is the end
Of Solomon Grundy.

Baa, Baa, Black Sheep.

BAA, baa; black sheep,
Have you any wool?
Yes, marry, have I
Three bags full;
One for my master,
And one for my dame,
But none for the little boy
Who cries in the lane.

Bell-Horses, Bell-Horses.

BELL HORSES, bell-horses,
What time of day?
One o'clock, two o'clock,
Off and away.

Baa, Baa Black Sheep.

As I Went over Lincoln Bridge.

AS I went over Lincoln Bridge,
I met Mister Rusticap;
Pins and needles on his back,
A-going to Thorney Fair.

(*A hedgehog.*)

Snail, Snail.

SNAIL, snail, come out of your hole,
Or else I will beat you as black as a coal.

Three Wise Men.

THREE wise men of Gotham
Went to sea in a bowl;
And if the bowl had been stronger,
My song would have been longer.

A Little Boy Went into a Barn.

A LITTLE boy went into a barn,
And lay down on some hay;
An owl came out and flew about,
And the little boy ran away.

Peter White.

PETER WHITE will ne'er go right.
Would you know the reason why?
He follows his nose wherever he goes,
And that stands all awry.

LITTLE Polly Flinders
Sat among the cinders,
    Warming her pretty little toes!
Her mother came and caught her,
And scolded her little daughter
    For spoiling her nice new clothes!

LEG over leg,

As the dog went to Dover;

When he came to a stile,

Hop he went over.

Little Girl, Little Girl.

LITTLE girl, little girl, where have you been?
Gathering roses to give to the queen.
Little girl, little girl, what gave she you?
She gave me a diamond as big as my shoe.

Little Robin Redbreast.

LITTLE Robin Redbreast sat upon a tree,
Up went Pussy cat, and down went he;
Down came Pussy cat, and away Robin ran;
Says little Robin Redbreast, "Catch me if you can."

Little Robin Redbreast jumped upon a wall,
Pussy cat jumped after him, and almost got a fall.
Little Robin chirped and sang, and what did Pussy say?
Pussy cat said, "Mew," and Robin jumped away.

What Shoemaker makes.

WHAT shoemaker makes shoes without leather,
With all the four elements put together?
Fire and water, earth and air;
Every customer has two pair.

Old Woman, Old Woman.

OLD woman, old woman, shall we go a-shearing?
"Speak a little louder, sir, I am very thick of hearing."
Old woman, old woman, shall I love you dearly?
"Thank you, kind sir, I hear you very clearly."

The Cuckoo's a Fine Bird.

THE cuckoo's a fine bird,
 He sings as he flies;
He brings us good tidings,
 He tells us no lies.

He sucks little birds' eggs,
 To make his voice clear;
And when he sings "cuckoo!"
 The summer is near.

Georgie Porgie.

GEORGIE Porgie, pudding and pie,
Kissed the girls and made them cry;
When the girls began to cry,
Georgie Porgie runs away.

Little Jack Nory.

LITTLE Jack Nory
Told me a story.
How he tried
Cock-horse to ride,
Sword and scabbard by his side,
Saddle, leaden spurs, and switches,
 His pocket tight
 With pence all bright,
Marbles, tops, puzzles, props,
Now he's put in a jacket and breeches.

Deedle, Deedle, Dumpling.

DEEDLE, deedle, dumpling, my son John,
He went to bed with his stockings on;
One stocking off, and one stocking on,
Deedle, deedle, dumpling, my son John.

A Long-tailed Pig.

A LONG-TAILED pig, or a short-tailed pig,
　Or a pig without e'er a tail,
A sow-pig, or a boar-pig,
　Or a pig with a curly tail.

Master I Have.

Master I have, and I am his man,
　Gallop a dreary dun;
Master I have, and I am his man,
And I'll get a wife as fast as I can,
With a heighly, gaily, gamberally,
Higgledy, piggledy, niggledy, niggledy,
　Gallop a dreary dun.

Old Mother Hubbard.

OLD Mother Hubbard
  Went to the cupboard,
To get her poor dog a bone;
But when she came there,
The cupboard was bare,
And so the poor dog had none.

She went to the baker's
  To buy him some bread;
But when she came back,
  The poor dog was dead.

She went to the joiner's
  To buy him a coffin;
    But when she came back.
    The poor dog was laughing.

She took a clean dish
 To get him some tripe;
But when she came back,
 He was smoking his pipe.

She went to the fishmonger's
 To buy him some fish;.
And when she came back,
 He was licking the dish.

She went to the ale-house
 To get him some beer;
But when she came back,
 The dog sat in a chair.

She went to the tavern
 For white wine and red;
  But when she came back,
  The dog stood on his head.

· She went to the hatter's
  To buy him a hat;
But when she came back,
 He was feeding the cat.

She went to the barber's
 To buy him a wig;
But when she came back,
 He was dancing a jig.

She went to the fruiterer's
　　To buy him some fruit;
But when she came back,
　　He was playing the flute.

She went to the tailor's
　　To buy him a coat;
But when she came back,
　　He was riding a goat.

She went to the cobbler's
　　To buy him some shoes;
But when she came back,
　　He was reading the news.

She went to the seamstress
　　To buy him some linen;
But when she came back,
　　The dog was spinning.

She went to the hosier's
　　To buy him some hose;
But when she came back,
　　He was dressed in his clothes.

The dame made a curtsey,
　　The dog made a bow;
The dame said, "Your servant,"
　　The dog said, "Bow, wow."

Old Mother Hubbard.

A Farmer Went Trotting.

A FARMER went trotting
Upon his grey mare,
  Bumpety, bumpety, bump!
With his daughter behind him,
So rosy and fair,
  Lumpety, lumpety, lump!

A raven cried "Croak! "
And they all tumbled down,
  Bumpety, bumpety, bump!
The mare broke her knees,
And the farmer his crown,
  Lumpety, lumpety, lump!

The mischievous raven
Flew laughing away,
  Bumpety, bumpety, bump!
And vowed he would serve them
The same next day,
  Lumpety, lumpety, lump!

Black We Are.

BLACK we are, but much admired;
Men seek for us till they are tired;
We tire the horse, but comfort man;
Tell me this riddle if you can.
                    (*Coals.*)

Old King Cole.

OLD King Cole
Was a merry old soul,
And a merry old soul was he;

He called for his pipe,
And he called for his bowl,
And he called for his fiddlers three.

Every fiddler, he had a fiddle,
And a very fine fiddle had he;
Twee tweedle dee, tweedle dee, went the fiddlers.

Oh, there's none so rare,
As can compare
With King Cole and his fiddlers three!

See, Saw, Margery Daw.

SEE, saw Margery Daw,
The old hen flew over the malt-house;
She counted her chickens one by one,
Still she missed the little white one,
And this is it, this is it, this is it.

Snail Snail.

SNAIL, snail, shut out your horns;
   Father and mother are dead;
Brother and sister are in the back-yard,
   Begging for barley bread.

As Soft as Silk.

As soft as silk, as white as milk,
As bitter as gall, a thick wall,
And a green coat covers me all.   (*A walnut.*)

Go to Bed, Tom.

Go to bed, Tom, go to bed, Tom—
Merry or sober, go to bed, Tom.

Up Hill, spare Me.

UP hill spare me,
Down hill 'ware me,
On level ground spare me not,
And in the stable forget me not.

Bless You, Bless You.

BLESS you, bless you, burnie bee;
Say, when will your wedding be?
If it be to-morrow day,
Take your wings and fly away.

Ding Dong Bell.

DING dong bell,
Pussy's in the well
Who put her in ?—
Little Johnny Green.
Who pulled her out ?—
Big Johnny Stout.
What a naughty boy was that
To drown poor pussy cat,
Who never did him any harm,
But killed the mice in his father's barn!

A Little Cock-Sparrow.

A LITTLE cock-sparrow sat on a tree,
Looking as happy as happy could be,
Till a boy came by, with his bow and arrow.
Says he, "I will shoot the little cock-sparrow.
His body will make me a nice little stew,
And his giblets will make me a little pie, too."
Says the little cock-sparrow, "I'll be shot if I stay,"
So he clapped his wings, and flew away.

DING DONG BELL

Mistress Mary, quite contrary, How does your garden grow?

Mistress Mary.

MISTRESS Mary, quite contrary,
    How does your garden grow?
With cockle-shells, and silver bells,
    And pretty maids all in a row.

Handy Spandy.

HANDY SPANDY, Jack-a-dandy,
Loved plum cake and sugar candy;
He bought some at a grocer's shop,
And out he came, hop, hop, hop.

About the Bush, Willy.

ABOUT the bush, Willy
 About the bee-hive,
About the bush, Willy,
 I'll meet thee alive.
Then to my ten shillings
 Add you but a groat,
I'll go to Newcastle,
 And buy a new coat.
Five and five shillings
 Five and a crown;
Five and five shillings,
 Will buy a new gown.
Five and five shillings,
 Five and a groat;
Five and five shillings
 Will buy a new coat.

Robert Barnes.

"ROBERT BARNES, fellow fine,
Can you shoe this horse of mine?"
"Yes, good sir, that I can,
As well as any other man:
Here a nail, and there a prod,
And now, good sir, your horse is shod."

Poor Old Robinson Crusoe.

POOR old Robinson Crusoe!
Poor old Robinson Crusoe!
They made him a coat
Of an old nanny-goat,
I wonder how they could do so!
With a ring-a-ting tang,
And a ring-a-ting tang,
Poor old Robinson Crusoe!

Ride, Baby, Ride.

RIDE, baby, ride,
Pretty baby shall ride,
And have a little puppy-dog tied to her side,
And a little pussy-cat tied to her other,
And away she shall ride to see her grandmother,
To see her grandmother,
To see her grandmother.

One, Two, Three, Four, Five.

ONE, two, three, four, five,
I caught a fish alive.
Why did you let it go ?—
Because it bit my finger so.

Little Maid, Pretty Maid.

LITTLE maid, pretty maid, whither goest thou?
"Down in the forest to milk my cow."
Shall I go with thee ?" No, not now;
When I send for thee, then come thou."

Pit, Pat, Well-a-Day.

PIT, pat, well-a-day,
Little Robin flew away;
Where can little Robin be ?—
Gone into the cherry-tree.

Eggs, Butter, Bread.

EGGS, butter, bread,
Stick, stock, stone dead!
Stick him up, stick him down,
Stick him in the old man's crown!

Dlddledy, Diddledy, Dumpty.

DIDDLEDY, diddledy, dumpty;
The cat ran up the plum-tree.
    I'll lay you a crown
    I'll fetch you down;
So diddledy, diddledy, dumpty.

Pussy Sits beside the Fire.

Pussy sits beside the fire,
    How can she be fair?
In comes the little dog,
    "Pussy, are you there?
So, so, dear Mistress Pussy,
    Pray tell! me how do you do?
"Thank you, thank you, little dog,
    I'm very well just now."

HUSHY, baby, my doll, I pray you don't cry,

And I'll give you some bread

and some milk by-and-by;

Or perhaps you like custard,

    or may-be a tart.

Then to either

you're welcome,

    with all my

        whole heart.

A Was an Archer.

 WAS an Archer, and shot at a frog;
B was a Butcher, and had a great dog.

C was a Captain, all covered with lace;
D was a Drunkard, and had a red face.

E was an Esquire, with pride on his brow;
F was a Farmer, and followed the plough.

G was a Gamester, who had but ill-luck;
H was a Hunter, and hunted a buck.

I was an Inn-keeper, who loved to bouse;
J was a joiner, and built up a house.

K was King William once governed this land;
L was a Lady, who had a white hand.

M was a Miser, and hoarded up gold;
N was a Nobleman, gallant and bold.

O was an Oyster-wench, and went about town;
P was a Parson, and wore a black gown.

A Was an Archer, and shot at a frog.

Q was a Queen, who was fond of good flip;
R was a Robber, and wanted a whip.

S was a Sailor, and spent all he got;
T was a Tinker, and mended a pot.

U was a Usurer, a miserable elf;
V was a Vintner, who drank all himself.

W was a Watchman, and guarded the door;
X was eXpensive, and so became poor.

Y was a Youth, that did not love school;
Z was a Zany, a poor, harmless fool.

Miss Jane had a Bag.

MISS JANE had a bag, and a mouse was in it,
She opened the bag, he was out in a minute.
The cat saw him jump, and run under the table,
And the dog said, "Catch him, puss, soon as you're able".

I Had a Little Dog.

I HAD a little dog, and they called him Buff;
I sent him to the shop for a hap'orth of snuff;
But he lost the bag and spilled the snuff,
So take that cuff, and that's enough.

"Croak!" said the Toad.

C ROAK!" said the toad, "I'm hungry, I think;
To-day I've had nothing to eat or to drink
I'll crawl to a garden and jump through the pales,
And there I'll dine nicely on slugs and on snails."

"Ho, ho!" quoth the frog, "is that what you mean?
Then I'll hop away to the next meadow stream;
There I will drink, and eat worms and slugs too,
And then I shall have a good dinner like you."

"Eleven
Elephants
Elegantly
Equipped"

OF all the gay birds
    that e'er I did see,
The owl is the fairest
    by far to me;
by far to me;
For all the day long
she sits on a tree,
And when the night comes,
    away flies she.

One Old Oxford Ox.

ONE old Oxford ox opening oysters;

Two tee-totums totally tired of trying to trot to Tadbury;

Three tall tigers tippling tenpenny tea;

Four fat friars fanning fainting flies;

Five frippy Frenchmen foolishly fishing for flies;

Six sportsmen shooting snipes;

Seven Severn salmons swallowing shrimps;

Eight Englishmen eagerly examining Europe;

Nine nimble noblemen nibbling nonpareils;

Ten tinkers tinkling upon ten tin
tinder-boxes with tenpenny tacks;

Eleven elephants elegantly equipped;

Twelve typographical topographers typically translating types.

The Babes in the Wood.

MY dear, do you know,
  How a long time ago,
Two poor little children,
  Whose names I don't know,
Were stolen away
  On a fine summer's day,
And left in a wood,
  As I've heard people say.

And when it was night,
  So sad was their plight,
The sun it went down,
  And the moon gave no light!
They sobbed, and they sighed,
  And they bitterly cried,
And the poor little things,
  They lay down and died.

And when they were dead,
  The Robins so red
Brought strawberry leaves,
  And over them spread;
And all the day long,
  They sung them this song:
"Poor babes in the wood! poor babes in the wood!
And don't you remember the babes in the wood ?"

The Babes in the Wood.

Hey, My Kitten.

HEY, my kitten, my kitten,
And hey, my kitten, my deary!
Such a sweet pet as this
Was neither far nor neary.

Little Jack Jingle.

LITTLE Jack Jingle,
He used to live single;
But when he got tired of this kind of life,
He left off being single, and lived with his wife.

Cock Robin.

COCK ROBIN got up early,
At the break of day,
And went to Jenny's window,
To sing a roundelay.

He sang Cock Robin's love
To the pretty Jenny Wren,
And when he got unto the end,
Then he began again.

Smiling Girls.

SMILING girls, rosy boys,
Come and buy my little toys;
Monkeys made of gingerbread,
And sugar horses painted red.

Darby and Joan.

DARBY and Joan were dressed in black,
Sword and buckle behind their back;
Foot for foot, and knee for knee,
Turn about, Darby's company!

My Maid Mary.

MY maid Mary;
She minds her dairy,
While I go hoeing and mowing each morn,
Merrily run the reel
And the little spinning-wheel,
Whilst I am singing and mowing my corn.

Little Robin Redbreast.

LITTLE Robin Redbreast
 Sat upon a rail;
Niddle naddle went his head,
 Wiggle waggle went his tail.

Mother, I Shall Be Married!

MOTHER, I shall be married
to Mr. Punchinello,
To Mr. Punch,
To Mr. Joe,
To Mr. Nell,
To Mr. Who,
Mr. Punch, Mr. Joe,
Mr. Nell, Mr. Who,
To Mr. Punchinello.

One, Two, Three, I Love Coffee.

ONE, two, three,
I love coffee,
And Billy loves tea.
How good you be!
One, two, three,
I love coffee,
And Billy loves tea.

Little Poll Parrott.

LITTLE Poll Parrot
Sat in her garret,
Eating toast and tea;
A little brown mouse,
Jumped into the house,
And stole it all away.

Tom, Tom.

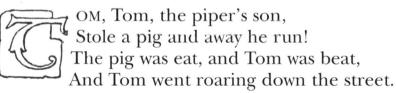

Tom, Tom, the piper's son,
Stole a pig and away he run!
The pig was eat, and Tom was beat,
And Tom went roaring down the street.

Eye Winker, Tom Tinker.

Eye winker,
Tom tinker,
   Nose dropper,
Mouth eater,
Chin chopper,
   Chin chopper.

THERE was a little boy and a little girl
    Lived in an alley;
Says the little boy to the little girl,
    "Shall I, oh! shall I?"

Says the little girl to the little boy,
    "What shall we do ?"
Says the little boy to the little girl,
    "I will kiss you."

My Father Left Me Three Acres of Land.

M Y father left me three acres of land,
　　Sing ivy, sing ivy;
My father left me three acres of land,
　　Sing holly, go whistle, and ivy!

I ploughed it with a ram's horn,
　　Sing Ivy, sing Ivy;
And sowed it all over with one peppercorn,
　　Sing holly, go whistle, and ivy!

I harrowed it with a bramble bush,
　　Sing ivy, sing ivy;
And reaped it with my little penknife,
　　Sing holly, go whistle, and ivy!

I got the mice to carry it to the barn,
　　Sing ivy, sing ivy;
And thrashed it with a goose's quill,
　　Sing holly, go whistle, and ivy!

I got the cat to carry it to the mill,
　　Sing ivy, sing ivy;
The miller he swore he would have her paw,
And the cat she swore she would scratch his face,
　　Sing holly, go whistle, and ivy!

A Carrion Crow.

A CARRION crow sat on an oak,
Fol de riddle, lol de riddle, hi ding do.
watching a tailor shape his cloak;
Sing heigh ho, the carrion crow,
Fol de riddle, lol de riddle, hi ding do.

Wife, bring me my old bent bow,
Fol de riddle, lol de riddle, hi ding do,
That I may shoot yon carrion crow;
Sing heigh ho, the carrion crow,
Fol de riddle, lol de riddle, hi ding do.

The tailor he shot, and missed his mark,
Fol de riddle, lol de riddle, hi ding do,
And shot his own sow quite through the heart;
Sing heigh ho, the carrion crow,
Fol de riddle, lol de riddle, hi ding do.

Wife, bring brandy in a spoon,
Fol de riddle, lol de riddle,
                    hi ding do
For our old sow is in a swoon;
Sing heigh ho, the carrion crow,
Fol de riddle, lol de riddle,
                    hi ding do.

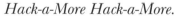

Hack-a-More Hack-a-More.

HICK-A-MORE, Hack-a-more,
On the King's kitchen-door;
All the King's horses,
And all the King's men,
Couldn't drive Hick-a-more, Hack-a-more,
Off the King's kitchen-door!
               (*Sunshine.*)

My Father He Died.

Y father he died, but I can't tell you how;
He left me six horses to drive in my plough;
With my wing, wang, waddle O,
   Jack sing saddle O,
   Blowsey boys bubble O,
     Under the broom.

I sold my six horses, and bought me a cow,
I'd fain have made a fortune, but did not know how;
   With my, etc.

I sold my cow, and I bought me a calf;
I'd fain have made a fortune, but lost the best half;
   With my, etc.

I sold my calf, and bought me a cat;
A pretty thing she was, in my chimney sat;
   With my, etc.

I sold my cat, and bought me a mouse;
He carried fire in his tail, and burnt down my house;
   With my, etc.

My Grandmother Sent.

MY grandmother sent me a new-fashioned three-cornered cambric country-cut handkerchief. Not an old-fashioned three-cornered cambric country-cut handkerchief, but a new-fashioned three-cornered cambric country-cut handkerchief.

THREE little kittens lost their mittens,

And they began to cry:

"O mother dear, we very much fear

That we have lost our mittens."

"Lost your mittens, you naughty kittens!

Then you shall have no pie."

"Mee-ow, mee-ow, mee-ow!

And we can have no pie.

Mee-ow, mee-ow, mee-ow!"

When I Was a Little Boy.

WHEN I was a little boy,
  I lived by myself,
And all the bread and cheese I got
  I put upon the shelf.

The rats and the mice
  They made such a life,
I was forced to go to London town
  To buy me a wife.

The streets were so broad,
  And the lanes were so narrow,
I could not get my wife home
  In a wheelbarrow.

The wheelbarrow broke,
  And my wife got a fall,
Down came the wheelbarrow,
  Wife, and all.

There Was an Old Woman.

THERE was an old woman of Leeds,
Who spent all her time in good deeds;
  She worked for the poor
  Till her fingers were sore,
This pious old woman of Leeds!

Old Mother Goose.

OLD Mother Goose, when
She wanted to wander,
Would ride through the air
On a very fine gander.

Mother Goose had a house,
'Twas built in a wood,
Where an owl at the door
For sentinel stood.

This is her son Jack,
A plain-looking lad;
He is not very good,
Nor yet very bad.

She sent him to market,
A live goose he bought,
"Here, Mother," says he,
It will not go for nought."

Jack's goose and her gander
Grew very fond;
They'd both eat together,
Or swim in one pond.

Jack found one morning,
As I have been told,
His goose had laid him
An egg of pure gold.

Jack rode to his mother,
The news for to tell,
She called him a good boy,
And said it was well.

Jack sold his gold egg
To a rogue,
Who cheated him out of
The half of his due.

Then Jack went a-courting
A lady so gay,
As fair as the lily,
And sweet as the May.

The rogue and the Squire
Came behind his back,
And began to belabour
The sides of poor Jack.

Then old Mother Goose
That instant came in,
And turned her son Jack
Into famed Harlequin.

She then, with her wand,
Touched the, lady so fine,
And turned her at once,
Into sweet Columbine.

The gold egg into the sea
  Was thrown then,—
When Jack jumped in,
  And got the egg back again.

The rogue got the goose,
  Which he vowed he would kill,
Resolving at once
  His pockets to fill.

Jack's Mother came in,
  And caught the goose soon,
And, mounting its back,
  Flew up to the moon.

I Had Two Pigeons.

I HAD two pigeons bright and gay;
They flew from me the other day;
What was the reason they did go?
I cannot tell, for I do not know.

THE Dog will come
      when he is called,
The Cat will walk away ;-
      The Monkey's cheek
         is very bald;
    The Goat is fond of play.
The Parrot is a
      prate-apace,
Yet knows not
      what he says:
The noble Horse
      will win the race,
Or draw you in a chaise.

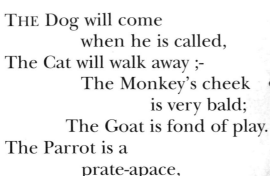

    The Sparrow steals the cherry ripe,
      The Elephant is wise,
    The Blackbird charms you with his pipe,
      The false Hyaena cries,
    The Hen guards well her little chicks,
      The Cow her hoof is slit,
    The Beaver builds
      with mud and sticks.
           The Lapwing
           cries
             "Peewit."

There Was a Little Guinea-Pig.

 HERE was a little Guinea-pig
Who, being little, was not big,
He always walked upon his feet,
And never fasted when he ate.

When from a place he ran away,
He never at that place did stay
And while he ran, as I am told,
He ne'er stood still for young or old.

He often squeaked and sometimes vi'lent,
And when he squeaked he ne'er was silent;
Though ne'er instructed by a cat,
He knew a mouse was not a rat.

One day, as I am certified,
He took a whim and fairly died;
And, as I'm told by men of sense,
He never has been living since.

Oh, That I Was Where I Would Be!

OH, that I was whcre I would be!
Then would I be where I am not!
But where I am I must be,
And where I would be I cannot.

There Was an Owl.

THERE was an owl lived in an oak,
   Wisky, wasky, weedle;
And every word he ever spoke,
   Was fiddle, faddle, feedle.

A gunner chanced to come that way,
   Wisky, wasky, weedle;
Says he, "I'll shoot you, silly bird,"
   Fiddle, faddle, feedle.

Come, My Children, Come Away.

COME; my children, come away,
For the sun shines bright to-day;
Little children, come with me,
Birds and brooks and posies see;
Get your hats and come away,
For it is a pleasant day.

Everything is laughing, singing,
All the pretty flowers are springing;
See the kitten, full of fun,
Sporting in the brilliant sun;
Children too may sport and play,
For it is a pleasant day.

Bring the hoop, and bring the ball,
Come with happy faces all;
Let us make a merry ring,
Talk and laugh, and dance and sing.
Quickly, quickly, come away,
For it is a pleasant day.

They that Wash on Monday.

THEY that wash on Monday
    Have all the week to dry;
They that wash on Tuesday
    Are not so much awry;
They that wash on Wednesday,
    Are not so much to blame;
They that wash on Thursday
    Wash for shame;
They that wash on Friday
    Wash in need;
And they that wash on Saturday,
    Oh! they're sluts indeed.

Danty Baby Diddy.

DANTY baby diddy,
What can a mammy do wid'e,
    But sit in a lap,
    And give 'un a pap?
Sing danty baby diddy.

Who Ever Saw a Rabbit?

WHO ever saw a rabbit
    Dressed in a riding-habit,
Gallop off to see her friends,in this style?
    I should not be surprised
    If my lady is capsized,
Before she has ridden half a mile.

"*Those who wash on Monday.*"

A for the Ape.

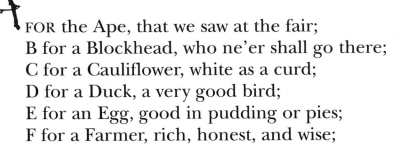

A FOR the Ape, that we saw at the fair;
B for a Blockhead, who ne'er shall go there;
C for a Cauliflower, white as a curd;
D for a Duck, a very good bird;
E for an Egg, good in pudding or pies;
F for a Farmer, rich, honest, and wise;

G for a Gentleman, void of all care,
I I for the Hound, that ran down the hare;
I for an Indian, in a grand chair;
K for the keeper, that looked to the park;
L for a Lark, that soared in the air;
M for a Mole, that ne'er could get there;

N for Sir Nobody, ever in fault;
O for an Otter, that ne'er could be caught;
P for a Pudding, stuck full of plums;
Q was for Quartering it—see, here he comes;
R for a Rook, that croaked in the trees;
S for a Sailor, that ploughed the deep seas;

T for a Top, that doth prettily spin;
V for a Virgin of delicate mien;
W for Wealth, in gold, silver, and pence;
X for old Xenophon, noted for sense;
Y for the Yew, which for ever is green;
Z for the Zebra, that belongs to the queen.

Oh, the Little Rusty, Dusty, Rusty Miller!.

OH, the little rusty, dusty, rusty miller!
I'll not change my wife for either gold or siller.

There Was an Old Woman.

THERE was an old woman who lived in a shoe,
She had so many children she didn't know what to do;

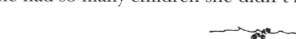

She gave them some broth without any bread;
She scolded them all soundly, and put them to bed.

Four-and- Twenty Tailors.

FOUR-AND-TWENTY tailors went to kill a snail,
The best man among them durst not touch her tail;
She put out her horns like a little Kyloe cow—
Run, tailors, run, or she'll kill you all e'en now.

When I Was a Little Girl.

WHEN I was a little girl, I washed my mammy's dishes;
Now I am a great girl, I roll in golden riches.

She gave them some broth without any bread.

"I'll Tell you a story."

I'll Tell You a Story.

I'LL tell you a story
About Jack a Nory—
And now my story's begun.
I'll tell you another
About Jack, his brother,
And now my story's done.

One, Two, Buckle My Shoe.

ONE, two,
Buckle my shoe;
Three, four,
Shut the door;
Five, six,
Pick up sticks;
Seven, eight,
Lay them straight;
Nine, ten,
A good fat hen;
Eleven, twelve,
Who will delve?
Thirteen, fourteen,
Maids a-courting;
Fifteen, sixteen,
Maids a-kissing;
Seventeen, eighteen,
Maids a-waiting;
Nineteen, twenty,
My stomach's empty.

The Miller He Grinds his Corn.

THE miller he grinds his corn, his corn
The miller he grinds his corn, his corn;
The Little Boy Blue comes winding his horn,
With a hop, step, and a jump.

The carter he whistles aside his team;
The carter he whistles aside his team;
And Dolly comes tripping with the nice clouted cream,
  With a hop, step, and a jump.

The nightingale sings when we're at rest;
The nightingale sings when we're at rest;
The little bird climbs the tree for his nest,
  With a hop, step, and a jump.

The damsels are churning for curds and whey;
The damsels are churning for curds and whey;
The lads in the fields are making the hay,
  With a hop, step, and a jump.

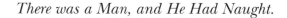

There was a Man, and He Had Naught.

HERE was a man, and he had naught,
And robbers came to rob him;
He crept up to the chimney-pot,
And then they thought they had him.

But he got down on t'other side
And then they could not find him;
He ran fourteen miles in fifteen days,
And never looked behind him.

Up Street, and Down Street.

UP street, and down street,
Each window's made of glass;
If you go to Tommy Tickler's house,
You'll find a pretty lass.

Ring-a-Ring-a-Roses.

RING-a-ring-a-roses,
A pocketful of posies;
Hush—hush—hush,
We'll all tumble down.

There Was an Old Crow.

THERE was an old crow
Sat upon a clod;
There's an end of my song
That's odd!

Tweedle-dum and Tweedle-dee.

TWEEDLE DUM and Tweedle-dee
Resolved to have a battle,
For Tweedle-dum said Tweedle-dee
Had spoiled his nice new rattle.
Just then flew by a monstrous crow,
As big as a tar-barrel,
Which frightened both the heroes so,
They quite forgot their quarrel.

Ring-a-ring o' roses.

To Market, To Market.

To market, to market, to buy a fat pig,
Home again, home again, dancing a jig;
Ride to market to buy a fat hog,
Home again, home again, jiggetyjog;
To market, to market, to buy a plum bull,
Home again, home again, market is done.

We're All in the Dumps.

E'RE all in the dumps,
    For diamonds are trumps,
The kittens are gone to St. Paul's!
    The babies are bit,
    The moon's in a fit,
And the houses are built without walls.

The Rose is Red.

THE rose is red, the violet blue,
The gillyflower sweet,—and so are you.
These are the words you bade me say
For a pair of new gloves on Easter-day.

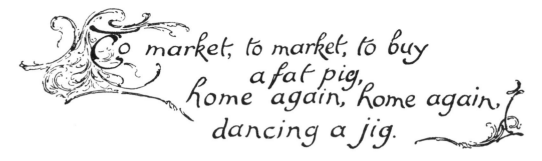

To market, to market, to buy
a fat pig,
home again, home again,
dancing a jig.

Pat-a- Cake, Pat-a- Cake.

PAT-A-CAKE, pat-a-cake, baker's man!
So I will, master, as fast as I can:

Pat it, and prick it, and mark it with T,
Put it in the oven for Tommy and me.

THREE straws on a staff,
would make a baby cry and laugh.

O Make Your Candles Last.

O make your candles last for aye,
　You wives and maids give ear-o
To put 'em out's the only way,
　Says honest John Boldero.

Tommy Trot.

TOMMY TROT a man of law,
Sold his bed and lay upon straw;
Sold the straw and slept on grass,
To buy his wife a looking-glass.

There Were two Blackbirds.

THERE were two blackbirds
　Sitting on a hill,
The one named Jack,
　The other named Jill;
Fly away, Jack!
　Fly away, Jill!
Come again, Jack!
　Come again, Jill!

There was an Old Man.

THERE was an old man of Tobago,
Who lived on rice, gruel, and sago;
　Till, much to his bliss,
　His physician said this,—
"To a leg, sir, of mutton you may go."

SWAN swam over the sea—
Swim, swan, swim;
Swan swam back again,
Well swum, swan.

The winds they did blow.

THE winds they did blow,
The leaves they did wag;
Along came a beggar-boy,
And put me in his bag.

He took me up to London,
A lady did me buy;
Put me in a silver cage,
And hung me up on high.

With apples by the fire,
And nuts for to crack;
Besides a little feather-bed,
To rest my little back.

Shoe the Colt, Shoe!

HOE the colt, shoe!
 Shoe the wild mare,
Put a sack on her back,
 See if she'll bear,
If she'll bear
 We'll give her some grains;
If she won't bear,
 We'll put on some reins!

You Shall Have an Apple.

You shall have an apple,
 You shall have a plum,
You shall have a rattle basket,
 When your dad comes home.

There Were Two Birds.

THERE were two birds sat on a stone,
 Fa la, la, la, lal, de;
One flew away, and then there was one,
 Fa, la, la, la, lal, de;
The other flew after, and then there was none
Fa, la, la, la, lal, de;
 And so the poor stone was left all alone,
Fa, la, la, la, lal, de!

Three Children Sliding on the Ice.

THREE children sliding on the ice
　　Upon a summer's day;
As it fell out, they all fell in,
　　The rest they ran away.

Now had these children been at home,
　　Or sliding on dry ground,
Ten thousand pounds to one penny
　　They had not all been drowned.

You parents all that children have,
　　And you that have got none,
If you would have them safe abroad,
　　Pray keep them safe at home.

Ride a Cock-Horse.

RIDE a cock-horse to Banbury-cross
To see an old lady upon a white horse,
Rings on her fingers, and bells on her toes,
And so she makes music wherever she goes.

What Are Little Boys Made of?

WHAT are little boys made of, made of?
What are little boys made of?
Snaps and snails, and puppy-dogs' tails;
And that's what little boys are made of, made of.

What are little girls made of, made of?
What are little girls made of?
Sugar and, spice, and all that's nice;
And that's what little girls are made of, made of.

When The Wind is in the East.

WHEN the wind is in the east,
'Tis neither good for man nor beast;
When the wind is in the north,
The skilful fisher goes not forth;
When the wind is in the south,
It blows the bait in the fishes' mouth;
When the wind is in the west,
Then 'tis at the very best.

Ride a cock horse to Banbury Cross.

There Was an Old Woman.

HERE was an old woman
        tossed up in a basket
Seventy times as high as the moon;
   where she was going I couldn't but ask it,
For in her hand she carried a broom.

"Old woman, old woman, old woman," quoth I,
  "O whither, O whither, O whither so high?"
"To brush the cobwebs off the sky!
  And I will be back again by-and-by."

When V and I Together Meet.

WHEN V and I together meet,
They make the number Six complete.
When I with V doth meet once more,
Then 'tis they Two can make but Four.
And when that V from I is gone,
Alas! poor I can make but One.

Three Blind Mice.

THREE blind mice, see how they run!
They all ran after the farmer's wife,
Who cut off their tails with the carving-knife.
Did you ever see such fools in your life?
Three blind mice.

Wash Me and Comb Me.

WASH me, and comb me,
And lay me down softly,
And set me on a bank to dry;
That I may look pretty
When some one comes by.

The House that Jack Built.

THIS is the house that Jack built.

This is the malt
That lay in the house that Jack built.

This is the rat,
That ate the malt
That lay in the house that Jack built.

This is the cat,
That killed the rat,
That ate the malt
That lay in the house that Jack built.

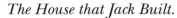

This is the dog,
That worried the cat,
That killed the rat,
That ate the malt
That lay in the house that Jack built.

This is the cow
       with the crumpled horn,
That tossed the dog,
That worried the cat,
That killed the rat,
That ate the malt
That lay in the house that Jack built.

This is the maiden all forlorn,
That milked the cow
       with the crumpled horn,
That tossed the dog,
T hat worried the cat,
That killed the rat,
That ate the malt
That lay in the house that Jack built.

This is the man
All tattered and torn,
That kissed the maiden
  all forlorn,
That milked the cow
  with the crumpled horn,

That tossed the dog,
That worried the cat,
That killed the rat,
That ate the malt
That lay in the house that Jack built.

This is the priest
  all shaven and shorn,
That married the man
  all tattered and torn,
That kissed the maiden
  All forlorn
    That milked the cow with the
      crumpled horn,

That tossed the dog,
That worried the cat,
That killed the rat,
That ate the malt
That lay in the house that Jack built.

This is the cock that crowed
        in the morn.
That waked the priest
        all shaven and shorn,
That married the man
        all tattered and torn,
That kissed the maiden all forlorn,
That milked the cow with the crumpled horn,
That tossed the dog,
That worried the cat,
That killed the rat,
That ate the malt
That lay in the house that Jack built.

This is the farmer sowing his corn,
That kept the cock that crowed in the morn,
That waked the priest all shaven and shorn,
That married the man all tattered and torn,
That kissed the maiden all forlorn.
That milked the cow,
        with the crumpled horn,
That tossed the dog,
That worried the cat,
That killed the rat,
That ate the malt
That lay in the house that Jack built.

All on a Summer's Morning.

Willy, Willy Wilkin.

WILLY, Willy Wilkin
Kissed the maids a-milking,
                    Fa, la, la!
And with his merry daffing,
He set them all a-laughing,
                    Ha, ha, ha!

Thirty days Hath September.

THIRTY days hath September,
April, June, and November;
February has twenty-eight alone,
All the rest have thirty-one,
Excepting leap-year—that's the time
When February's days are twenty-nine.

Come, Dance a Jig.

COME, dance a jig
To my granny's pig,
With a raudy, rowdy, dowdy;
Come, dance a jig
To my granny's pig,
And pussy-cat shall crowdy.

March Winds.

MARCH winds and April showers
Bring forth May flowers.

Where Have You Been All the Day?

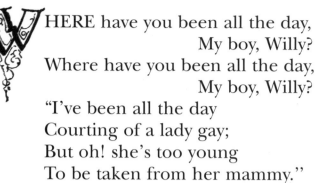

WHERE have you been all the day,
          My boy, Willy?
Where have you been all the day,
          My boy, Willy?
"I've been all the day
Courting of a lady gay;
But oh! she's too young
To be taken from her mammy."

What work can she do,
          My boy, Willy?
Can she bake and can she brew,
          My boy, Willy?
"She can brew and she can bake,
And she can make our wedding-cake;
But oh! she's too young
To be taken from her mammy."

What age may she be,
          My boy, Willy?
What age may she be,
          My boy, Willy?
"Twice two, twice seven,
Twice ten, twice eleven;
But oh! she's too young
To be taken from her mammy."

Wee Willie Winkie.

WEE Willie Winkie
Runs through the town,
Up-stairs and down-stairs,
In his night-gown;
Tapping at the window,
Crying at the lock,
"Are the babes in their bed ?
For it's now ten o'clock."

When Good king Arthur.

HEN good King Arthur ruled this land,
He was a goodly king;
He stole three pecks of barley-meal,
To make a bag-pudding.

A bag-pudding the king did make,
And stuffed it well with plums:
And in it put great lumps of fat,
As big as my two thumbs.

The king and queen did eat thereof
And noblemen beside;
And what they could not eat that night
The queen next morning fried.

Little Jack Dandy-prat.

LITTLE Jack Dandy-prat was my first suitor;
He had a dish and a spoon, and he'd some pewter;
He'd linen and woollen, and woollen and linen,
A little pig in a string cost him five shilling.

Thomas and Annis.

HOMAS and Annis met in the dark.
  "Good morning," said Thomas;
"Good morning," said Annis;
  And so they began to talk.

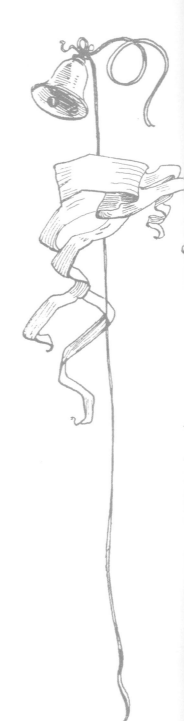

"I'll give you," said Thomas.
  "Give me!" said Annis;
"I prithee, love, tell me what?"
  "Some nuts," said Thomas.
' Some nuts," said Annis;
  "Nuts are good to crack."

"I love you," said Thomas.
  Love me!" said Annis;
"I prithee, love, tell me where?"
  "In my heart," said Thomas.
"In your heart!" said Annis;
  "How came you to love me there?"

"I'll marry you," said Thomas.
  "Marry me!" said Annis;
"I prithee, love, tell me when ?"
  "Next Sunday," said Thomas.
"Next Sunday," said Annis;
  "I wish next Sunday were come."

IF I had a donkey that wouldn't go,

Wouldn't I wallop him? Oh, no, no!

GOOSEY, Goosey Gander,

Who stands yonder?

Little Betsy Baker;

Take her up, and shake her.

There was an old Woman.

THERE was an old woman, as I've heard tell,-
She went to market her eggs for to sell;
She went to market all on a market-day,
And she fell asleep on the king's highway.

There came by a peddler whose name was Stott,
He cut her petticoats all round about;
He cut her petticoats up to her knees,
Which made the old woman to shiver and freeze.

When this little woman first did wake,
She began to shiver and she began to shake;
She began to wonder and she began to cry,
"Oh I deary, deary me, this is none of I!"

"But if it be I, as I do hope it be,
I've a little dog at home, and he'll know me;
If it be I, he'll wag his little tail,
And if it be not I, he'll loudly bark and wail."

Home went the little woman all in the dark,
Up got the little dog, and he began to bark;
He began to bark, so she began to cry,
"Oh I deary, deary me, this is none of I"!

A-Milking, A-Milking.

A-MILKING, a-milking, my maid.
"Cow, take care of your heels," she said,
"And you shall have some nice new hay,
If you'll quietly let me milk away."

Dogs in the Garden.

DOGS in the garden, catch 'em, Towser;
Cows in the cornfield, run, boys, run;
Cats in the cream-pot, run, girls, run, girls;
Fire on the mountains, run, boys, run.

"POLLY, put the kettle on,

And let's drink tea."

BLOW, wind, blow, and go, mill, go,

That the miller may grind his corn;

That the baker may take it,

And into rolls make it,

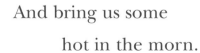

And bring us some

hot in the morn.

Polly, put the Kettle On.

 OLLY, put the kettle on,
Polly, put the kettle on,
Polly, put the kettle on,
And let's drink tea.

Sukey, take it off again,
Sukey, take it off again,
Sukey, take it off again,
They're all gone away.

Little Tee Wee.

LITTLE Tee Wee,
He went to sea
In an open boat;
And while afloat
The little boat bended,
And my story's ended.

I Like Little Pussy.

I LIKE little pussy,
Her coat is so warm,
And if I don't hurt her,
She'll do me no harm;
So I'll not pull her tail,
Nor drive her away,
But Pussy and!
Very gently will play.

The Three Jovial Huntsmen.

HERE were three jovial Huntsmen,
  As I have heard them say,
And they would go a-hunting
  Upon St. David's Day.

All the day they hunted, -
  And nothing could they find,
But a ship a-sailing,
  A-sailing with the wind.

One said it was a ship,
  The other he said, Nay;
The third said it was a house,
  With the chimney blown away.

And all the night they hunted,
And nothing could they find
But the moon a-gliding,
A-gliding with the wind.

One said it was the moon,
The other he said, Nay;
The third said it was a cheese,
And half o't cut away.

And all the day they hunted,
And nothing could they find -
But a hedgehog in, a bramble-bush,
And that they left behind.

The first said it was a hedgehog,
The second he said, Nay;
The third it was a pin-cushion,
And the pins stuck in wrong way

And all the night they hunted,
And nothing could they find,
But a hare in a turnip-field
And that they left behind.

The first said it was a hare,
The second he said, Nay;
The third said it was a calf,
And the cow had run away.

And all the day they hunted,
And nothing could they find
But an owl in a holly-tree,
And that they left behind.

One said it was an owl,
The other he said, Nay;
The third said 'twas an old man,
And his beard growing gray.

Rock-a-By, Baby, thy Cradle is Green.

ROCK-A-BY, baby, thy cradle is green;
Father's a nobleman, mother's a queen;
And Betty's a lady, and wears a gold ring;
And Johnny's a drummer, and drums for the king.

Hush-a-by, baby, on the tree top,
When the wind blows the cradle will rock.
When the bough bends, the cradle will fall—
Down will come baby, bough, cradle, and all.

Rock-a-by, Baby.

There Was a Monkey.

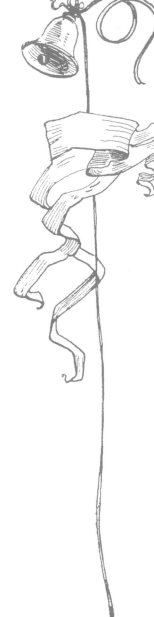

HERE was a monkey climbed up a tree;
When he fell down. then down fell he.

There was a crow sat on a stone;
When he was gone, then there was none.

There was an old wife did eat an apple;
When she had eat two, she had eat a couple.

There was a horse going to the mill,
When he went on, he stood not still.

There was a butcher cut his thumb;
When it did bleed. then blood did come.

There was a lackey ran a race;
When he ran fast he ran apace.

There was a cobbler clouting shoon;
When they were mended, they were done.

There was a chandler making candle;
When he them strip, he did them handle.

There was a navy went into Spain,
When it returned, it came again.

This Pig Went to Market.

1. THIS pig went to market;
2. This pig stayed at home;
3. This pig had a bit of meat;
4. And this pig had none;
5. This pig said, "Wee, wee, wee!
   I can't find my way home."

The Rose is Red.

THE rose is red, the grass is green;
And in this book my name is seen.

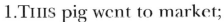

Brow brinky,

Eye winky,

Chin choppy;

Nose noppy,

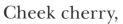

Cheek cherry,

Mouth merry.

Ladybird, ladybird, fly away home,
Thy house is on fire, thy children all gone,
All but one, and her name is Ann,
And she crept under the pudding pan.

Rain, Rain, Go Away.

RAIN, rain, go away;
Come again another day;
Little Harry wants to play.

There was a Piper.

THERE was a piper had a cow
    And he'd no hay to give her.
He took his pipe, and played a tune
    Consider cow consider!

The cow considered very well,
    For she gave the piper a penny,
That he might play the tune again
    Of "Corn rigs are bonnie!"

There was a piper.

Jack Sprat.

JACK SPRAT could eat no fat,
His wife could eat no lean,
And so between them both
They licked the platter clean.

Jack ate all the lean,
Joan ate all the fat,
The bone they picked clean,
And gave it to the cat.

When Jack Sprat was young,
He dressed very smart:
He courted Joan Cole,
And captured her heart.

In his fine leather doublet,
And greasy old hat,
Oh! what a smart fellow
Was little Jack Sprat.

"Oh, what a smart fellow".

Joan Cole had a hole
In her new petticoat;
To get her a patch,
Jack gave her a groat.
The groat bought a patch,
Which covered the hole:
"I thank you, Jack Sprat,"
Said little Joan Cole.

Jack Sprat was the bride-
groom,
Joan Cole was the bride;
Jack said from the church
His wife home should ride.
But no coach could take her,
The lane was so narrow.
Said Jack, "Then I'll take her
Home in a wheelbarrow."

As Jack Sprat was wheeling
His wife by the ditch,
The barrow turn'd over,
And in she did pitch. Says
Jack, "She'll be drown'd!"
But his Joan made reply,
"I don't think I shall,
For the ditch is quite dry."

Jack brought home his Joan,
And she sat in a chair,
When in came his pussy,
Who had but one ear.
Says Joan,
"I'm come home, Puss,
Pray how do you do?"
The cat wagged her tail,
But said nothing but "Mew!"

Jack Sprat took his gun
And went to the brook:
He aimed at the drake
But he slaughtered the duck.

He brought it to Joan,
Who a fire did make
To roast the fat duck,
While Jack went for the
drake.

The drake swam around
With his nice curly tail,
Jack Sprat came to shoot him
But happened to fail.

He let off his gun
But went wide of the mark:
The drake flew away
With a mocking
Quack! Quack!

Jack Sprat to live pretty
Now bought him a pig;
It was not very little
Nor yet very big.
It was not very lean,
It was not very fat;
"T'will serve for a grunter,"
Said Little Jack Sprat.

Jack Sprat bought a cow
His Joan for to please,
For Joan she could make
Splendid butter and cheese,
Or pancakes or puddings
Without any fat;
A notable housewife
Was little Joan Sprat.

Jack and Joan went abroad,
Puss took care of the house;
She caught a large rat,
And a very small mouse.

She caught a small mouse,
And a very large rat;
"You're an excellent hunter,"
Says Little Jack Sprat.

"You're an excellent hunter."

Now Jack has got rich.

Jack Sprat went to market
And bought him a mare;
She was lame of three legs,
And her ribs they were bare.
She was blind of both eyes,
And the mare had no fat,
"She looks like a racer,"
Says Little Jack Sprat.

Now I've told you the story
Of Little Jack Sprat,

And of Little Joan Cole
And the poor one- eared cat.
Now Jack loved his Joan
And some good things
he taught her;
Then she gave him a son
And a dear little daughter.
Now Jack has got rich,
And has plenty of pelf,
If you know any more,
You may tell it yourself.

Jack and Jill.

JACK AND JILL went up the hill
To fetch a pail of water;
Jack fell down
and broke his crown,
And Jill came tumbling after.

Then up Jack got and home
did trot
As fast as he could caper;
Dame Gill did the job
to plaster his head
With vinegar and brown
paper.

Jack and Jill.

Then Jill came in and she did grin
To see Jack's paper plaster.
Her mother scolded her across the room
For laughing at Jack's disaster.

This made Jill pout and she ran out,
And Jack did quickly follow:
They rode dog Ball, Jill got a fall,
How Jack did laugh and holloa!

Dame Gill did grin
as she went in,
And Jill was plagued by Jack.
Will Goat came by and
made Jack cry,
And knocked him on his
back.

Now Jill did laugh
and Jack did cry,
But his tears did soon abate.
Then Jill did say
that they should play
At see-saw across the gate.
They see-sawed high,
they see-sawed low,
At length they both did
tumble;
      "We both are down
        we both must own,
      Let neither of us
      grumble."

They see-sawed low.

Then the next thing they made a swing, But Jill set up a big
cry, For the swing gave way in the midst of the play,
And threw her into the pigstye.

The sow came by,
says Jack –"I'll try
If I can't ride this prancer!"
He jumped with a whack
on old Sow's back,
But she led him a droll
dance, Sir!

Sow ran and squalled
while Jack he bawled,
And Jill joined in the choir.
Dog Ball, being near,
bit Sow by the ear,
And threw Jack in the mire.

On old sow's back.

Though Jack was not hurt,
he was all over dirt,
I wish you had but seen him,
And Jill did jump
with him to the pump,
And pumped on him to clean
him.
Hearing the rout
Dame Gill came out,

With a horse-whip from the
door;
She laid it on Jack and poor
Jill's back,
Until they both did roar.
Ball held Sow's ear and both
in rear
Rang against old Dame and
hit her,

He was all over dirt.

That she did fall o'er Sow and Ball,
How Jack and Jill did twitter.
And now all three went in to see
To put the place to right-all;
Which done they sup,
then drink a cup,
And wish you a good-night all.

A good-night all.

Little Red Riding hood.

ONCE upon a time, in a cottage near a wood, there lived a pretty little girl. Her grandmother, who lived on the other side of the wood, had made a beautiful red hood for her, and everybody called her 'Red Riding-Hood'.

One day her mother said to Red Riding-Hood: "My dear, your grandmother has been ill, so I want you to go and see if she is better, and take her some nice things in this basket.

"Go straight along the road; do not play or idle, and do not talk to any one."
But Red Riding-Hood went through the wood,

thinking it by far the prettier way, and in the wood she met an old wolf.

Now this wolf wanted to eat her, but was afraid, because of some woodcutters not far off, so he asked her where she was going, and got her to tell him all about her grandmother.

When the wolf had found out all he wanted to know, he ran as fast as he could towards the grandmother's cottage. But Red Riding-Hood, finding it very pleasant in the wood, dawdled along, picking flowers here and gathering nuts there, making posies, and chasing butterflies.

Little Red Riding Hood.

Meantime the wolf had reached the cottage and knocked gently on the door. The grandmother asked who it was, and, speaking in a squeaky voice, he pretended to be Red Riding-Hood. Hearing that, the grandmother, who was in bed, called out; "Pull the bobbin,and the latch will go up."

And the wolf did as she said. the door then opened, and the wolf rushed into the cottage, and, springing on the old woman, gobbled her up, for he had eaten nothing for a long time, and was very hungry. Then he shut the door, and, putting on the grand-mother's nightgown, nightcap and spectacles, got

into bed to wait for Red Riding-Hood.

He had not long to wait. In a little while the child came tapping at the door, and the wolf, making his voice as soft as possible, told her to pull the bobbin, lift the latch and enter.

When she stepped into the cottage, the wolf covered himself up well in the bed-clothes, and told her to sit beside him.

So Red Riding-Hood sat down, but when she saw how strange her granny looked, she said:

He knocked gently.

"Oh, grandmamma, what great arms you have got!"

"All the better to hug you, my dear."

Red Riding-Hood then said:

"Oh, grandmamma, what great ears and eyes you have got!" "All the better to hear and see you, my dear."

Red Riding-Hood looked again and then said:

"Oh, grandmamma, what great teeth you have got!"

"All the better to eat you, my dear!" said the wolf, and sprang up in bed to seize the little girl, and gobble her up.

He covered himself up well.

But at that moment a wood-cutter who was Red Riding-Hood's father, and had come to take her home, peeped in at the window and saw the wolf springing out of the bed.

He quickly ran in and soon chopped off the wicked wolf's head with his axe. Then he lifted poor Red Riding-Hood in his arms. The little girl was very much frightened, and threw her arms round her father's neck and cried

bitterly. Then the woodcutter, holding her very tightly to make her feel quite safe, carried her home.

And as he went along he sang to her these wise words:

"A little maid must be afraid
To do other than her mother
told her;
Of idling must be wary, of
gossiping be chary, she'll
learn prudence by the time
that she is older."